FOR THE BIRDS
Crosswords

by
ANDREW J. RIES

PUBLICATIONS
Adventure
an imprint of Adventure**KEEN**

DEDICATION

To my mother

ACKNOWLEDGEMENTS

This book would not have been possible without the generous contributions of many people. In particular, I'd like to thank David Plotkin and Neville Fogarty for their diligence in test-solving the puzzles and giving their valuable feedback. In addition, countless family members and friends have continued to provide their love and support through this project. I have deep gratitude to everyone who made this book possible.

Cover and book design by Lora Westberg

10 9 8 7 6 5 4 3

Copyright @ 2013 by Andrew J. Ries
Published by Adventure Publications
An imprint of AdventureKEEN
310 Garfield Street South
Cambridge, MN 55008
(800) 678-7006
www.adventurepublications.net

ISBN 978-1-59193-380-9 (pbk.)

INTRODUCTION

"For the birds," "birds of a feather flock together," "the early bird gets the worm"—these are just a few of the many colorful phrases in the English lexicon that our feathered friends have inspired. When I started this project, I was grateful to have such a wealth of material available to craft some clever puzzles that honor the world of birds.

Now I'm not here to try to stump you by asking you the average number of feathers on a golden eagle's left wing, or which genus of fly a flycatcher prefers. This book is made for a wide range of crossword enthusiasts—diehard daily solvers and casual solvers alike. In addition, bird enthusiasts can appreciate a chance to flex their avian knowledge, pencil in hand.

The clues and entries offered in this book include lively, interesting and fun facts about birds. While not every clue could be bird-related, roughly one-quarter of the clues do relate to birds in one way or another. Of course, all the themes in this book are centered on birds, real and fictional. So feel free to enjoy these puzzles while relaxing on the back porch, doing some bird-watching on a Saturday morning.

—A.J.R.

CROSSWORD CONSTRUCTION 101

Constructing a good crossword puzzle is a scientific art. The best crosswords have solid themes in which wordplay and linguistic trickery have been employed in exquisite ways that can only be described as artistic. Yet even the greatest crossword "artists" must adhere to the science of construction. Since the 1940s, crossword puzzles have had a set of rigid guidelines that standardize construction and, in a sense, provide the frame on which the artist can showcase his work. These rules include:

1) Symmetry. All crosswords must have a symmetrical positioning of black squares. For most puzzles, this symmetry is rotational; that is, if you turn the grid upside down, the arrangement of black squares will stay the same.

2) Word count. Though this rule may change depending on the publisher, a good rule of thumb for a standard 15x15-square puzzle is that there is a maximum of 78 entries in the grid. The puzzles in this book use the 78 maximum word count in 15x15 puzzles, and a 98 maximum word count for 17x17 puzzles.

3) All-interlocking design. No one square can be "unchecked"; that is, every across square must have a down counterpart, and vice versa. Also, the grid cannot have any "isolated" sections that are blocked off from the rest of the grid.

4) No two-letter words. Three letters are the minimum length for an entry.

5) Black square count. Roughly no more than one-sixth of a grid's squares can be black squares. For a 15x15 puzzle, this means about 38 black squares. This is probably the most flexible rule, but puzzles with more than 42 black squares are pushing it.

Of course, all rules are meant to be broken. But for the most part, these rules are the standard in American crosswords, and the puzzles that follow adhere to these style guidelines. Nevertheless, not all crosswords that abide by these rules are automatically "good" puzzles. This is where the artist comes into play. As mentioned, a strong theme is at the crux of a quality crossword. The use of flashier letters—think of the high-value Scrabble letters like Q, Z, X and J—makes a puzzle more visually appealing than one flooded with E's and N's and S's. But, like art, the final result is ultimately up to the individual to judge. My hope is that you judge these puzzles positively.

FOR THE BIRDS
Crosswords

SYMBOLIC FLIERS

Going "postal" with the circled squares in this puzzle.

ACROSS

1 *Purple ___
6 Avoid a puddle, flamboyantly
10 "Woodstock" supergroup, initially
14 Oil giant whose headquarters is now the Aon Center
15 Hughes poem that references Whitman
16 Mayberry young 'un
17 *Western ___
19 Shed feathers
20 Flight start approx.
21 Sylvester, to Tweety
22 White Owl Cigars competitor
24 Went like the Roadrunner
26 *Northern ___
29 Military members act on them
31 Winger of *Legal Eagles*
32 Without any change
35 SEC powerhouse
36 Provide assurance to a lender, in a way
37 Call ___ career (retire)
38 *Brown ___
40 Haul around clumsily
41 They haven't been seen in Mauritius since the seventeenth century
43 Steel wool brand
44 Club with warblers
45 Kagan on the Supreme Court
46 Source of some grainy YouTube videos
48 *Mountain ___
50 Crafty, like Dickens' Dodger
54 English Breakfast go-with
55 Central Oklahoma city
56 Alicia of *Falcon Crest*
57 Frozen drink brand with a blue raspberry flavor
59 Legislature-recognized symbols that the answers to the starred clues are, in relation to the abbreviation represented in their circled squares
62 "Wacky" diver on Canadian currency
63 Emulate a myna
64 Corset features
65 Barn owl's spot, maybe
66 Comparative word often misspelled
67 Hot Chile month

DOWN

1 Having big status
2 "___ man with seven wives . . ."
3 Policy of many non-profit websites
4 Included in on an e-mail
5 Owl, vocally
6 Vireo's song, e.g.
7 Hellenic H
8 Tubes that run down the abdomen
9 Game where twos are slangily called ducks
10 Extreme left-wingers, in dated slang
11 Wader with a distinctive beak
12 Zilch
13 To date
18 Walks like a penguin
23 Newly built wing, e.g.
25 Weed chopper
26 Flew on auto-pilot
27 Engage in debate
28 Jessica of *Blue Sky*
30 Foreign exchange student's course, maybe
32 Cassette half
33 Key chain?
34 Availed
36 Fall in buckets
38 Bryson who sang the theme from *Aladdin*
39 He may sing a swan song?
42 Gumball price (at least when I was young)
44 Global clock std.
46 Pathetic sort
47 Like Corn Belt soil, mostly
49 Detailed atlas frame
51 The Marx Brothers' *Duck Soup*, for one
52 Gambler's alternative for the over
53 Calf roping need
55 Bevies and bevies
57 Suffering from chicken pox, say
58 Pigeon call
60 "Oh, *that's* what you mean"
61 *Goldeneye* author Fleming

Answers on page 48

THE BIRDS AND THE B'S
This puzzle doesn't sting.

ACROSS

1 They may be learned with song lyrics
5 Hair on an eyelid
9 Like a place swarming with activity
14 Bench press target, briefly
15 Start the kitty
16 *Flight of the Intruder* star Willem
17 God, to Giles
18 Vanderbilt and Harriman, for two
20 African nation whose flag features a grey crowned crane
22 "Mr. Blue Sky" gp.
23 "The wolf ___ the door"
24 Pioneer in paperback publishing
27 Edit menu button
28 Part of a Mountie's outfit
32 Arabian Peninsula gulf or city
35 *Kite Stories* musician Brian
37 2011 animated film whose title character is a chameleon
38 Sty female
39 It's used for prying
42 Framed stuff
43 Model of perfection
45 Wing that doesn't flap?
46 Fencing blade
47 Like wares in one's garage, often
50 Warrior described in *The Iliad*
52 Neologism that originated during the 2004 presidential campaign
57 Off the fence, perhaps
60 Advanced 42-Across deg.
61 Vultures, vis-à-vis vireos
62 Physical reaction to fear
65 Jai ___ (game played in round-robin format)
66 Eschew method-style acting, say
67 Certain style of a bird feeder
68 Bird feeder kernel
69 Like a birdbrain
70 North Carolina school whose sports teams are the Phoenix
71 Throw in the trash

DOWN

1 Make sense logically
2 Dull brownish color
3 Use a feather duster, perhaps
4 Non-lethal weapon that can bring you to your knees
5 Bo Jackson, as an NFLer
6 Melissa portrayer on *Falcon Crest*
7 Blue Jays' all-time wins leader Dave
8 Conversation starters
9 Computer language pioneer Lovelace
10 Espresso bar tender
11 Little green men pilot them, supposedly
12 Home to the football Cardinals, casually
13 Competitor of Dove soap
19 Ski bum's footwear
21 Dull brownish color
25 Jaywalking is one
26 Lancaster's roll-in-the-sand scene partner
29 "Dang, son!"
30 Monstrous figure
31 It may be high for a songbird
32 Valley girl's phrase of doubt
33 Stammering bird in Wonderland
34 Large water vessel
36 Have an obligation
39 Bird's digital protector
40 Flap one's jaw, say
41 "Swanee" hitmaker, 1920
44 Meadowlark Lemon stats
46 Draw out, like a mineral
48 Arboreal perch
49 Flow out
51 Good rating for a stock
53 Linguistic root of "pariah"
54 Home for Chilly Willy
55 Gets warmer, in a way
56 Reacts passively to a joke
57 No longer a spring chicken
58 City with a University of Alaska branch campus
59 Chilly Willy, for one
63 Very wide pump spec.
64 West Bank gp.

Answers on page 48

ALL TOGETHER NOW
This puzzle's not for loners.

ACROSS

1 Pick up a bird call
5 Open just a crack
9 Bricklayer's cart
12 Shepard of *Black Hawk Down*
15 A, in radio correspondence
16 Ranger Smith's nemesis
18 Lennon's squeeze
19 Group of cranes' frame of mind?
21 Bulk Camel purchase: Abbr.
22 Don't touch with a ten-foot pole, say
23 Yank
24 Mallards' homes
26 Bill passed by a group of owls?
31 Lioness "born free"
33 Bird's "sexy" counterpart?
34 Johnson nicknamed "The Rock"
35 Set of standards for a group of rooks?
40 Prepare duck confit, in part
41 *The Godfather* victim Luca
42 Objectively review
44 Title for Robert Byrd: Abbr.
45 Group of sparrows emcee the Academy Awards?
49 Eagle Scouts may lead it
52 Early delivery, for short
53 Peter of *The Raven*, 1963
55 Dovetail
58 Group of jays killing the buzz?
62 Nixon's eldest
64 Nixon met him in 1972
65 Philadelphia Eagles' division
66 Group of finches performs cohesively?
71 "As a result . . ."
72 Brokers may act on it
73 Try to discourage
76 Herbert of the *Pink Panther* series
77 Whodunit featuring a group of crows?
82 Mexican Mrs.
83 Detective's findings
84 Breezy "bye"
85 Rooster's mate
86 Knock quickly
87 Lippy response
88 "I hear ya"

DOWN

1 Response to a funny guy
2 2,301 ft., for Eagle Mountain (Minnesota's highest point)
3 Mixed-race ethnicity
4 Ultra right-wingers, e.g.
5 81-Down, on the high seas
6 Voight of *Return to Lonesome Dove*
7 Ten-percenter: Abbr.
8 It's slung at a rodeo
9 *Grey's Anatomy* star Katherine
10 Muffin morsel
11 Booze ban, i.e.
12 Common Pacific salmon type
13 "Stick" on a Firebird, e.g.
14 Popular job-listing website
17 Fuzzy image
20 Summertime setting in Denver: Abbr.
25 Stockpile
27 ___-Wan Kenobi
28 Egret's hangout
29 You can turn it to tune
30 They may be bright in Bordeaux?
31 Waves back?
32 Fly, for one
36 A-line designer
37 Point of editing
38 ___ Kosh B'Gosh
39 British mil. honor
43 Battle site of 1944
46 Brilliant part of a bird of paradise
47 Org. that awards Taylor Swift
48 Tire filler
49 Bird and Magic were on it
50 Bobbles a grounder, e.g.
51 Where to find chicks
52 Attacks, in cockfighting
54 Many a Strauss composition
55 Character actor in *Sling Blade*
56 It's heavily mined in northern Minnesota
57 Avian nickname of longtime prisoner Robert Stroud
59 Songbird Sumac
60 Super ___ (fundraising bloc)
61 "That sounds good!"
63 Chemist's related compound
67 Gadget for using an iPod on the road
68 Long-time Net Jason
69 Lunged weapons
70 Annoyance while playing *Angry Birds*
74 One-named Deco great
75 2012 candidate Paul
78 Sch. in the "Old Dominion"
79 Genetic letters
80 Between-acts fillers, briefly
81 "Affirmative"

Answers on page 46

LET'S GET QUACKING
Toon in to this puzzle.

ACROSS

1 Music maker for the flock
6 When the Orioles start the season, typically
11 Looking sickly
14 *Horse Feathers* horn-blower
15 "I Got a Name" folkie Jim
16 Waves back?
17 Catchphrase for 52-Across
20 Sphere that's a sib backwards
21 Before, to Rita Dove
22 Like one that's gone platinum?
23 Creator of 52-Across
26 Fruits and berries, for waxwings
29 Bray half
30 Added fuel to the fire
31 Play SPARROW in Scrabble, perhaps
32 Train station
35 University whose sports teams' logo features 52-Across
36 Celeb-chasing gossip show
39 One who doesn't need to ID to serve shots
41 Seattle-to-Reno dir.
42 52-Across' occupation, apparently
44 Like hot wings
46 Don Draper, for one
47 None of the Stanford Lady Cardinals
48 Airport pat down org.
51 Lee's soldiers, for short
52 Character that debuted in 1934's "The Wise Little Hen"
56 Wide, wavy tie
58 Far East philosophy
59 Decreased the feeder stash
60 Catchphrase for 52-Across
64 Crow's cousin
65 Dismissive look
66 Robin and Roo's creator
67 Birds ___ (frozen foods giant)
68 Birds found on the beach
69 Notable trait for the peregrine falcon

DOWN

1 "That's amazing!"
2 Ardently enthusiastic, say
3 Popular WWII-era pin-up girl Betty
4 Well-suited
5 Yellow-___ albatross
6 Wants in a desperate way
7 Tense start?
8 Said "Stick 'em up!"
9 With a mean streak
10 Brick that needs no mortar
11 Rites with two bands and a band?
12 *Fish* actor Vigoda
13 Org. whose members have large wingspans
18 Three, headed?
19 Film that won't play at megaplexes, say
24 Former Atlanta Hawks owner Turner
25 Web junkie, slangily
27 Self-worth psyches
28 Warbling quality
31 Troublemaker
33 Like Poe's raven, color-wise
34 A birdie beats it
35 Shootout preceders: Abbr.
36 King's old counterpart in Moscow
37 Whipped up
38 African country once called Southern Rhodesia
40 Bills are passed by them
43 Rodeo hoop
45 Balance sheet abbr.
47 ___ Goose
49 Legally vulnerable, perhaps
50 First part of a play
52 Blackmore's heroine
53 Put an egg in the nest
54 Condemns
55 Atwitter, with "up"
57 A dermatologist may cut it out
60 Praiseful song
61 Mr. Ed's fodder
62 Turkey-loving Franklin
63 Like one who wears skinny jeans and has a fauxhawk, apparently

Answers on page 47

DIFF'RENT STROKES
You may need to chip in on this one.

ACROSS

1 Practice some jabs
5 Anaheim Duck's tool
10 Relaxing retreats
14 Word on Irish coinage
15 Pang of pain
16 Rash reliever
17 Happy as a lark
18 Blender gasket, e.g.
19 One of the Canaries, e.g.
20 Flier that's three under [see circles], literally
22 Jay who wrote *The Amityville Horror*
23 Small ewe
24 Hall-of-Fame duffer at home in this puzzle
26 Gemologist's sides
29 "Little Sparrow" singer Dolly
30 ___-bellied flycatcher (yellow-brown bird)
31 Joe who won three Super Bowls coaching the Redskins
32 Gp. known for selling cookies
35 Don't mention it
36 Flier that's two under [see circles], literally
37 Long in the distance
38 *The Maltese Falcon* hero, for one
39 Horse feathers
40 Separated, say
41 With great interest
43 Flier that's one under [see circles], literally
44 There aren't any shores near it
46 Cruise in the middle of a 2012 custody battle
47 One side of an economic dichotomy
48 What each of the fliers in the puzzle is, in this puzzle
53 Purim's month
54 Purse snatcher, for one
55 Major Aussie export
56 Bar used to get a leg up
57 State of uncontrolled violence
58 Parasite dangerous to many birds
59 Like early levels of *Angry Birds*
60 Underground vault
61 Visualizes, either way you read it?

DOWN

1 Sonic the Hedgehog's maker
2 Dosage unit
3 Baghdad resident, e.g.
4 Signal used in a crisis
5 Birds lining up on power lines may predict them
6 Wave of pain
7 ___ lorikeet (flashy bird)
8 Starting rank at a British police squad
9 Frat party staple
10 Having had one too many cocktails, slangily
11 It's hot for only a short time
12 Pass out
13 Segment of *The Seagull*, e.g.
21 Where to see J. M. W. Turner's "Head of a Heron"
22 Paycheck figs.
25 Kill ___ killed
26 Webbed part of a duck
27 Fictional company used to thwart the Road Runner
28 Hall-of-Fame duffer at home in this puzzle
29 Toe, to a tot
31 Comedian known for smashing watermelons
33 Delhi gal's garb
34 Johnson of *Laugh-In* fame
36 One, in German
37 Fruits similar to plums
39 *Porgy and ___*
40 Puts on TV
42 Red Bull supplies it
43 All-you-can-eat restaurant
44 Blackhawks often land there
45 St. Anthony's city
46 Owls don't do it at night
49 Greasy
50 Redhead of '60s TV
51 Timed event
52 Antlered beasts
54 Cinephile's channel

Answers on page 46

CHILDISH NAMES
Don't brood over this puzzle.

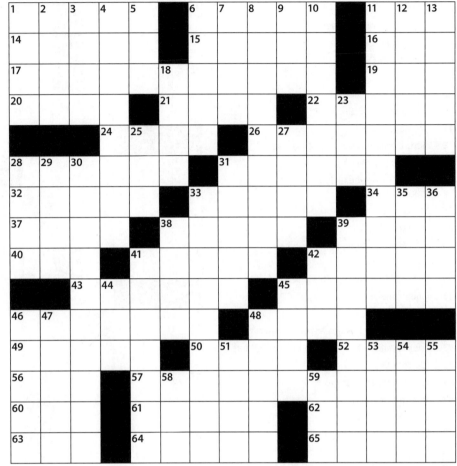

Answers on page 46

ACROSS

1 Hay storage sites

6 Scottish bodies of water

11 Pen's mate

14 Fitting nickname for the Pittsburgh Penguins' old arena, with "the"

15 Shady lane, in Lyon

16 Start of Montana's motto

17 Bobbed-hair gal of the '20s, familiarly [Swan]

19 Late-'90s boy band

20 Busy-season office worker

21 Clay pigeons are shot from it

22 Cigar tips?

24 Golf champ McIlroy

26 Break-the-bank winnings

28 Like a cell phone

31 Something to chew on for Fido, say

32 Precocious *Pygmalion* gal

33 Smallish jazz bands

34 Executes a Halloween prank, briefly

37 Winged goddess of victory

38 Offspring . . . whose specific names are at the beginning of 17-Across and 11-Down and the end of 30-Down and 57-Across

39 Tom Seaver's old stomping grounds

40 One-fourth of *quatre*

41 Specifically

42 Major Colorado brewery

43 Did a DEA bust

45 Mixed doubles game

46 Judy Garland's downfall, reportedly

48 "Do you mind?"

49 Frida whose self-portrait featured a hummingbird

50 College mil. program

52 Henpecks

56 NFL Cardinals, on scoreboards

57 *Drive* star, 2011 [Goose]

60 Nurse's skill, initially

61 Intro deliverer

62 Peace Nobelist Anwar

63 ["It's a bat!"]

64 Sushi bar cupfuls: Var.

65 Attacks a mosquito, say

DOWN

1 Force needed for flight

2 Make bedroom eyes at, say

3 Deception

4 Blue ribbon, perhaps

5 Use the dinner roll to pick up the gravy

6 Bird of Boston lore

7 Sprightly Korbut

8 Not-on-the-level business

9 That gal

10 Taps

11 Classic .357 Magnum revolver [Crane]

12 Operatic hero for Gluck

13 Give a leg up

18 Raison d'___

23 Result of a Pacquiao pow?: Abbr.

25 Commercial suffix for Motor-

27 Bug-eyed

28 Where to find duck and quail, perhaps

29 Lena of *Mr. Jones*

30 Leather-clad Harley driver, slangily [Nightingale]

31 Stonehenge worshiper of old

33 Bar in the bathroom

35 Roz portrayer on *Frasier*

36 Backtalk

38 Luke Skywalker's mentor

39 Daughter's husband's title

41 Cassiterite and others, geologically speaking

42 Ex-Dodger Ron, nicknamed "Penguin"

44 "You've got mail" co.

45 Burrito alternative

46 Chicago Blackhawk's footwear

47 Country singer Steve

48 Homeowner's onuses: Abbr.

51 "The ___ Love" (REM hit)

53 Slave for Verdi

54 Insect eaten by swallows

55 Some GI drillers: Abbr.

58 "Chicken Talk" singer Sumac

59 Draft org.

FLYING COLORS
Featuring some all-American birds

ACROSS

1 Cheryl of *Charlie's Angels*
5 Be a stool pigeon, say
9 Overflowing
14 Hose color
15 Caramel-filled candy
16 Alabama city in 1965 news
17 "If I may interject . . ."
18 Picture that may be double-clicked
19 Osprey's gripper
20 Colorful passerine nicknamed the "butcher bird"
23 "Rooster tail" of a motorboat
24 Pricey sparkler
25 *Duck Hunt* gaming platform
26 Four-door cars
29 Nicki called a "black Lady Gaga" by some
31 Funky-smelling
32 Birdies beat them
33 Word on many businesses' neon signs
37 Colorful falcon-like flier with black shoulders
40 "Can't help ya"
41 Takeoff guesses, for short
42 '90s Internet platform
43 Some zoo sounds
45 Enlisted man who may build docks
46 ___-relief
49 Chum, in Cherbourg
50 Give a derisive hoot
51 Colorful seabird whose name derives from the Spanish for "stupid"
57 Rangers All-Star pitcher Ogando
58 "Toodle-oo"
59 Hawaiian music accompaniers, for short
60 Barkeep's supply
61 "6 in the Mornin'" rapper
62 Roger Maris' number for the Cardinals
63 Angler's bait
64 Picnic throwaway
65 Target of a November hunt, maybe

DOWN

1 "The Owl and the Pussycat" poet
2 Pine (for)
3 ___ Scott Decision of 1857
4 It brings food to a new level?
5 Fire ring components
6 "Key" philosopher John?
7 ___ vera
8 Octopussy and Holly Goodhead, for two
9 Cause for wheezing
10 Don a chicken costume, e.g.
11 Card shark's ballsy move
12 Have a drag
13 Brand hawked by Michael Jordan
21 *Duck Dynasty* airer
22 Birdbrain's lack
26 Like cut lumber
27 Give a parrot's reply
28 Need a plumber's attention, as a pipe
29 Some hired help
30 Share a moment of levity
32 Devoted to the flag . . . like the three birds at 20-, 37-, and 51-Across?
34 Mr. ___ (Dr Pepper rival)
35 End of many female names
36 *Wild Things* co-star Campbell
38 Line in many Spanish romance films, say
39 Dorky type
44 Clumsy
45 Calm and composed
46 Atlanta Hawks' sport, briefly
47 Title TV role for Jane Curtin
48 Snide remark you best not make to a lawyer
50 Derek of the 3,000 hit club
52 Corporate kahuna, briefly
53 Snack with salsa
54 Dust Bowl nomad
55 The "B" of N. B.
56 River to the North Sea

Answers on page 47

SERVICE WITH A SIMILE

Featuring some avian expressions.

ACROSS

1 "Yikes!"
6 Oriole's position while hitting
12 Teasdale or Paretsky
16 Jules in a bookcase
17 So far
18 ___ the finish
19 "A little birdie told me . . ."
20 Totally off the map, to bird-lovers
22 Less bird-brained, as an idea
24 "I didn't need to know that," in text-speak
25 See red
26 In one's birthday suit, to bird-lovers
30 "Guy walks into ___ and says 'Ouch'"
32 Brisk air "feature"
33 *Birds & Blooms* VIPs
34 Sparrow's head?
35 Nurse Wild Turkey, say
36 Dough dispenser
37 Orange part of a sunbird
40 Ecstatic, to bird-lovers
43 Out of the office
47 *Peacock* star Page, 2010
48 Fond du ___, WI
49 The D of LED
50 No, in Novgorod
51 Having lost one's marbles, to bird-lovers
55 Shining brightly
57 Subj. of many '60s protests
58 2000 title role for Richard Gere
59 Ladera Ranch-to-San Juan Capistrano dir.
62 Brain scan letters
63 Seaside tourist spot
64 It doesn't have much of a point
65 Against violence, to bird-lovers
70 Scandal-plagued Houston firm
71 Sports org. that featured the Pittsburgh Condors
72 Weather report stat.
75 Prudent, to bird-lovers
79 Where a jess is tied during falconry
80 Panache
81 "Love Light in Flight" singer Wonder
82 Ed of the Reagan cabinet
83 Wets
84 Boob tubes
85 One making pitches for Bird's Eye, perhaps

DOWN

1 Roman poet who wrote *Ibis*
2 Nervous laughter
3 Sour Jolly Rancher flavor
4 Even (with)
5 Popular Yankee Jeter
6 Reg.
7 Basic maneuver for Astaire
8 Founding father who pushed for the bald eagle becoming the national bird
9 Sprightly Comaneci
10 San Francisco : BART :: Chicago : ___
11 Some MIT grads
12 Lesser-played half of a 45
13 Societal breakdown
14 Speed gaugers, e.g.
15 Like hawks and doves, politically speaking
21 Deep gorge
23 Oscar de la ___
27 Sets the mood with the lights
28 Boo bird's call
29 Aleutian city that's the westernmost in the U.S.
30 Sickly looking
31 Oniony bagel without a hole
36 John Galt creator Rand
37 Rage of flames
38 Like sexts
39 Showy part of a turkey
41 Org. that frowns upon birdcages
42 Trade name for banned spray daminozide
44 It has a long and strong bill
45 Love to death
46 *Fiddler on the Roof* matchmaker
49 Canoeing obstacle
51 Symbol that starts a score
52 Sauce brand for chicken parm
53 *Up in the Air* Oscar nominee Kendrick
54 NASDAQ competitor
56 Davis of *The Fly*
59 Erupted, like Etna
60 A little daffy from age
61 European capital known as the "phoenix city," due to its need to rebuild following battle
63 Negative response to being asked to go to a movie
64 Tied up the score
66 *Fargo* directing team
67 Where turkeys are rolled?
68 Flying higher than
69 Bowl-___
73 German river or valley (anagram of LIES)
74 Nestling's sound
76 Flier retired in 2003
77 Four wheeler, e.g., for short
78 ___ *Misérables*

Answers on page 48

TWEET-Y BIRDS

Get a "handle" on this one.

ACROSS

1. Jailbird's sentence, maybe
5. Batted, but didn't play the field
9. *Downton* ___
14. Tangy Minute Maid drink
16. Bird that dances to attract mates
17. @loopy_since1963: sometimes i think outside the box . . . but my nose keeps bringin me back!! It always knows ya know :) #passionfroot
18. Kept yakkin', say
19. Spike TV, formerly
20. Courage, metaphorically
21. Sonar sound
22. Birthright seller in Genesis
24. @wackyquacky: great newth! sounth like @huey37 @louie37 @dewey37 r on thr way to vithit me! cant wait #ohboyohboyohboy
28. Robin's egg blue, e.g.
30. Memorable time
31. Aunt Bee looked after him
32. Get dangerous, as winter roads
35. Jong who wrote *Fear of Flying*
37. MLK Day mo.
38. With 40-Across, @rule_the_Rooster: i say i say what a day! henhouse was crawlin w/ chix. now if i could only get that durn @georgeP_Dawg #doodah
40. See 38-Across
42. Spanish for "that"
43. DEA employees, slangily
45. Held in check
46. Turkey shoot need, briefly
48. Tic-tac-toe winner
49. Prime meridian setting: Abbr.
50. @CJblue_speeddemon49: whatcha got up ur sleeve now @Shop_Acme? #beepbeep
53. Showiness
57. "Hawks and Doves" rocker Young
58. Kermit the ___
60. One of a buzzard's pair?
61. Cheese with holes
63. @Sparky_secretary: long day at my typewriter @snoopdog_aviation gripe gripe gripe!!!!! zzzzzzzzzzzz hate workin 4 peanuts lol #whosurcaddy
65. Rental agreement
66. Noise law, for instance
67. *One Flew Over the Cuckoo's Nest* award
68. Sign of things to come
69. Birds Eye morsels

DOWN

1. Wife in *Being John Malkovich*
2. Clubs used on eagle shots, often
3. Flora and ___
4. SASE, e.g.
5. Strip naked
6. Is obligated by law, perhaps
7. *Up* voice actor
8. Byrd's party: Abbr.
9. Overly bitter
10. His *On the Waterfront* character keeps pigeons
11. Superb work, slangily
12. Coldplay producer Brian
13. Bread taken in Tokyo
15. Funny bit
21. Residential street
23. "No dice"
25. Seed coverings (LIARS anagram)
26. One-named R&B artist with the hit "1, 2 Step"
27. "You killed ___!" (*South Park* catchphrase)
29. Second word of "The Raven"
32. Lead-in to bad news
33. Vodka cocktail, familiarly
34. Self-centered person
35. Scandal-ridden Houston firm
36. Turkish royals
39. Diplomat Wallenberg
41. Modern address letters
44. Follow popular trends, e.g.
47. City in Ukraine or Texas
49. DeNiro's *Midnight Run* co-star
51. Choir platform part
52. Suffer from wind or rain, perhaps
54. Layer important to the atmosphere
55. Pilgrimage city
56. Toy dogs, for short
59. *Password* reruns airer
61. ___-mo replay
62. *Moonrise Kingdom* director Anderson
63. Turn on the charm, say
64. Keg part

Answers on page 48

BY THE NUMBERS
Dealing with some noted people here.

ACROSS

1 Attire worn while trussing a chicken, perhaps
6 One-ups
11 Like a wet hen, in a saying
14 Romantic muse
15 Much-debated 2010s legislation, casually
17 Fifty past the hour, put another way
18 *Bee Gees brother of Barry and Maurice
19 *Superman* co-star Beatty
20 Cub Scout kahuna
22 NHL all-star Kovalchuk
23 *Folkie who founded Righteous Babe Records
27 Many a "Stan," pre-1991: Abbr.
28 Intense anger
29 It means "both" at the beginning
31 Hawked wares, briefly
34 *"Ain't That a Kick in the Head?" crooner
40 Alessandro with an electrical unit named for him
42 Number of eggs a sparrow lays per day
43 Hooting, chirping, squawking, etc.
44 *Jazzy gal who performed on the second episode of *Saturday Night Live*
47 Was sure of
48 Brown-colored passerine
49 Level for the Toledo Mud Hens and Memphis Redbirds
51 Strapping young ___
53 *Country star famously interrupted by Kanye West
60 Composer Khachaturian
62 Awaits approval
63 Society page word
64 Fliers with vocal organs . . . and a hint to the answers to the starred clues?
67 Having taken the gas
69 Using holy water in a bird bath, e.g.
70 Makes muddy
71 Western state whose motto translates to "she flies with her own wings": Abbr.
72 Plagued with troubles
73 Clear from one's hard drive

DOWN

1 Hartford-based HMO
2 Emulate a peacock
3 Skeptical magician James
4 Missouri native
5 "That's cheating!"
6 Woodpecker, for one
7 Deadly African virus
8 Title-winning Alabama coach Nick
9 "Eww . . . gross!" initialism
10 ___ Juan Capistrano (annual swallow-returning site)
11 Goes through the motions, say
12 Fast food chain with horsey sauce
13 Shut out
16 *Rio* technology
21 Britney Spears' ex, slangily
24 One counting calories
25 Pheasant hunter's helper, briefly
26 Muscat's land
30 Tom of TV news
31 NBA honor
32 Simpsonian outburst
33 Awkward number during prom, say
35 Winged goddess of the dawn
36 Michelle's counterpart during the 2012 campaign
37 Anagram of 42-Across
38 Expert closing?
39 Hot off the press
41 Help out a jailbird, perhaps
45 Bambi's aunt
46 Loony bin section
50 Put one's fears to rest
51 Rodeo "weapon"
52 Like Red Wings fans after a goal
54 Strategic Belgian city during WWI
55 Pigeon's resting place
56 Very beginning
57 The blue peacock is its national bird
58 Does a textural analysis?
59 Like a man of few words
61 Orioles boss: Abbr.
65 Lobster joint clip-on
66 Dot in la mer
68 Neither fish ___ fowl

Answers on page 46

STUCK IN THE MIDDLE

In the answers to the starred clues, BIRD can follow the first half and precede the second half.

ACROSS

1 Punch in a tannery
4 Wannabe, in surfer slang
9 Ear-cleaning stick
13 Spring off the ground
15 Dr. Crane's sign
16 Perot or Stockdale's alma mater: Abbr.
17 *Casablanca* gal
18 Starr who co-wrote "Flying"
19 Rat-___
20 *Opening track of *Led Zeppelin IV*
22 Source of mescaline
24 Subj. with many x's and y's
25 Animated Chihuahua of the '90s
26 Shaker ___, OH
27 Rudimentary learning initials
28 Rack-clearing ploys in Scrabble
30 *Anthropologist's study
32 Brought KFC home, say
33 Normandy battle site
34 Former Hawk Phil, briefly
35 *Place for lawbreakers
38 Turkey is a part of it
41 Easter egg choices
42 It may air a filibuster
46 *No-charge talking-to?
48 "Beat it!"
49 "Bad Moon Rising" gp.
50 Ask personal questions, e.g.
51 *Three Days of the Condor* star Max ___ Sydow
52 Dairy farm beast
53 Sound like a canary
55 *Slow-dance selection
57 Falco of *Nurse Jackie*
58 Lightly fry
60 *Young Frankenstein* gal
61 Declump, as flour
62 Al Capp's "Lil" kid
63 Dumb as a ___
64 Diggs of *Private Practice*
65 Have a jones for
66 Jeanne d'Arc's title

DOWN

1 Classic character in Arabian folklore
2 Like the homes in Thomas Kinkaid paintings
3 Layered Italian entrée
4 Unruly flock
5 Layered bulb
6 "Wow that hurts!"
7 Insurer in much 2008–9 news
8 Pull a cheeky prank?
9 Anchoring place
10 Bad weather featuring claps, briefly
11 Caught by quail hunters, say
12 Longtime Penn State football coach Joe
14 Super ___ (fundraising bloc)
21 Swedish funds
23 Night school course, for short
26 Rings above some winged figures
29 Plastic fighter since 1964
30 Barrymore of *The White Raven*
31 "Good golly!"
33 Like a fox, say
36 "From my perspective . . ."
37 Starbucks snack
38 Division featuring Seahawks and Cardinals, briefly
39 Los Angeles suburb
40 Scare the pants off of
43 Pennsylvania vacation spot, with "The"
44 In the midst of
45 London prison in many Dickens novels
47 Klinger's rank: Abbr.
48 Rule the roost
51 One in a booth in November
54 ___ noire (pet peeve)
55 Pale-green moth
56 Nurse Grey Goose, say
59 Vigoda who voiced a penguin in 2007

Answers on page 48

GIVE ME A CALL
Sounds like these birds like this puzzle.

ACROSS

1 Did like Walter Lantz
5 Landing site in Washington State
11 ___ Tin Tin
14 The Hawkeyes of the Big Ten
15 Involve . . . or a typographical feature of "chicken"?
16 Blood typing syst.
17 Dove's favorite Paul Newman film?
19 Brit. honor first issued in 1914
20 Far-north natives
21 Baseball Hall-of-Famers Lombardi and Banks
23 Here-there connector
24 Goose's favorite Chinese region?
26 Groupon posting
29 "Smoking or ___?"
30 It's tapped out for help
31 Chicken king Sanders' rank: Abbr.
32 Supposed "missing links"
35 Fundraiser suffix
38 Owl's favorite TV catchphrase?
41 Foul smell
42 More gun-shy
43 37-Down employee
44 Give a moniker to
46 Bill word
47 Signed, as a contract
49 Crow's favorite astronomer?
52 General ___'s chicken
53 Top-of-the-line
54 South Asian guides
58 Allow
59 Duck's favorite anti-drug slogan?
62 Before, to Byron
63 *The Serpent's Egg* star Liv
64 Not 65-Across
65 Not 64-Across
66 Matter in one's will
67 Backwoods line of chivalry

DOWN

1 Prepare chicken for tacos, perhaps
2 Aussie hoppers
3 *Return of the Jedi* critter
4 Hawaiian surfer chick
5 Mexican mister
6 Winds (up)
7 Falcons' home, for short
8 Letter in the *Animal House* frat
9 *Cats and Bats and Things with Wings* poet Conrad
10 They man tills
11 Best Buy competitor
12 Henrik who penned *The Wild Duck*
13 "I'll pass on the post-meal headache"
18 Lacking a compass, say
22 Marky Mark group, initially
24 Four-bagger for an Oriole
25 Newborn's get-up
26 Eight, to Eduardo
27 Polly's cracker, e.g.
28 Overflow substance
29 One of two states whose state bird is the mountain bluebird
33 Comics onomatopoeia
34 Largest county in 29-Down
36 High-pitched double reed
37 Queens protectors, briefly
39 Tie up a turkey
40 Responds to a cuckoo clock, maybe
45 Whence "jai alai"
48 Its national bird is the white-throated dipper
49 Symbol on a score
50 Last Olds model
51 Ancient Franks
52 "For ___ is the kingdom . . ."
54 32-card bridge cousin
55 Transom piece
56 Emulates Hunt and Peck
57 2% alternative
60 Flight control meas.
61 Org. that may honor the Dixie Chicks

Answers on page 47

CHEEP SHOTS
Hope you can get the picture.

ACROSS

1. R&B group ___ Hill
4. Lexington acad.
7. Call from the crow's nest
11. Puts two and two together, e.g.
15. Goddess of the dawn
16. It's charged in physics class
17. Soothing Kleenex additive
18. Post-victory crow
19. *1989 Duvall-Jones Western miniseries
22. Tiny fraction of a newton
23. Wing: Prefix
24. Left-wing lawyer's org.
25. Oklahoma county in the title of a 2008 Tony-winning play
26. *1986 critical bomb co-starring Tim Robbins
30. Fish-fowl connector
31. Last part of 4-Across: Abbr.
32. Fast flier
33. Mythical weeper mentioned in Hamlet's soliloquy
35. Pompous sort
36. *2010 Oscar-winner for Natalie Portman
40. "___ Fideles" (Christmas carol)
44. Tennyson's "The Owl," for one
45. Major Samoan crop
46. *1940 Mae West-W.C. Fields comedy
50. George Eliot's *Adam* ___
51. Scholastic catch-all, briefly
52. Cosmetics giant
53. *1983 Lou Gossett Jr. film that spawned three sequels
56. Une, in Ulm
57. Rhea's role in *Cheers*
58. Global economic org.
59. Ravens rusher, e.g.
63. Cop's boss: Abbr.
65. *1941 Bogart thriller cited as the first *film noir*, with "The"
69. Coffee has a distinct one
71. Having wings
72. Motherly head?
73. Shipping deduction
74. Ornithologist's activity . . . and an alternate title for this puzzle?
77. Revered figure
78. Sanctuary section
79. A great deal
80. Bible book after Ezra: Abbr.
81. 2012 candidate Gingrich
82. Wildlife refuge
83. Site of stereotypically long lines, briefly
84. Thug's "piece"

DOWN

1. Famed oracle site
2. Be a cheerleader for, say
3. Monthly magazine that ditched its print version in 2010
4. Bill for a golfer
5. Holstein's sound
6. Jailbirds
7. Chicken soup server
8. Not under one's breath
9. Turkey Day mo.
10. Bustard's tail?
11. Gives a helping hand
12. Miami Heat star nicknamed "Flash"
13. Dog that preys on emus
14. Dismissive look
20. The "E" of Q.E.D.
21. German's "real"
25. "I get the picture"
27. Gig that involves spinning records, say
28. "A friend" in French
29. Obama's title, militarily speaking: Abbr.
34. Twinkler casually known as a "Betsy"
35. One with many a day in court, for short
36. Yard ball game: Var.
37. Book of Mormon prophet
38. Neighborhood
39. *Waiting in the Wings* playwright Coward
40. Both in front?
41. Textile colorist
42. *Loon Lake* novelist whose name evokes medicine
43. Touristy Tuscan town
44. ___ Grant (student aid)
47. Within one's rights
48. Spot for an aerie
49. ___-Tiki (Heyerdahl craft)
54. Humorist Bombeck
55. Yellowhammer State: Abbr.
56. "Precious" shade of green
58. "Vidi," to Caesar
59. Uninteresting
60. Peter Finch's specialty
61. It covers a pupil
62. "Giddy-up" chess piece
63. Shiny fabric
64. Chicken egg rating
66. Anklebones
67. Wise, respected one
68. *Mad Men* airer
70. Prepare butter for popcorn
74. The Orioles, on scoreboards
75. Frothy brew, for short
76. An older jake

Answers on page 46

SELLING POINTS
Celebrating some avian mascots.

ACROSS

1 Like boobies and buoys
5 Wing measurements
10 Korean golfer K. J.
14 Woodshop file
15 Lubricate
16 Oafish sort
17 Not buying one's B.S., say
18 Carne ___ (Mexican dish)
19 Blemishes for Eagles QBs
20 Navajo foe
21 Avian mascot of potato chips
23 Oregon city where *One Flew Over the Cuckoo's Nest* was filmed
25 Equal: Prefix
26 *The Crying Game* star Stephen
27 Avian mascot of car insurance
31 "Hark the Herald Angels Sing" and others
33 Look that can evoke a shiver
34 Cardinal's duds, slangily
35 Tarzan portrayer in the '60s
36 Avian mascot of the U.S. Forest Service
39 Biting one's nails et al.
42 Bed with casters
43 Their number can be determined in a Faraday cup
47 "A bird in the hand is worth two in the bush," for one
48 Avian mascot of fruity cereal
50 Nickelodeon dog, and a homophone of a songbird
51 Christopher Robin's pal
53 Dust-up
54 Avian mascot of pickles
59 Stool pigeon
60 "___ Kleine Nachtmusik"
61 It's meant only for the audience
62 What a penny symbolizes in a fountain
63 Finger sound
64 Add spice to, with "up"
65 Have some "barking dogs," say
66 "D" student's bane
67 Battery port
68 Leave the chicken on the grill too long, maybe

DOWN

1 Wake-up call purpose
2 State capital with much Spanish Mission-style architecture
3 George's mom on *Seinfeld*
4 Addr. on a care package
5 Fly like an eagle
6 City home to a leaning tower
7 Hawkeye portrayer
8 Annoying pest, in Yiddish slang
9 Fixes a feline
10 Ad man's prize
11 Surprised party at a surprise party, e.g.
12 Be a better hawker, say
13 "Have no fear"
21 Yukon automaker
22 Moody Blues hit of 1965
24 It's got two pairs of wings and pincers
28 Lewis and Martin, Batman and Robin, etc.
29 Grand Forks sch.
30 *The ___ Kid* ('50s western show)
32 Tweeting, perhaps
35 Coll. marching group
37 *SNL* alum Cheri
38 Eagles hit "I Can't Tell ___ Why"
39 Busy time for a farmer
40 "Sweet" girl of song
41 Crazy as a loon
44 Flightless bird prized for their feathers
45 Boris's animated partner
46 Apply liberally, as sauce
48 Add as a bonus
49 Pose a question
52 Central Florida city on the old Dixie Highway
55 National Chicken Month: Abbr
56 Modern recording device
57 Had a fatal dose of, for short
58 Russo who played 45-Down on screen in 2000
62 Seattle Redhawks' conf.

Answers on page 47

DROP IT!

I admit, it's kind of a crappy punchline.

ACROSS

1   Need a massage, maybe
5   ___, skip, and jump
9   Part of a Robin costume
13 2011 Chris Hemsworth role
14 Inflict upon
15 Firebirds move on them
16 *October Sky* actress
18 Assigns some stars to, perhaps
19 Start of a joke
21 Steering system bar
23 Merkel of *Summer and Smoke*
24 ___ Tin Tin
25 *Juno and the Paycock* has three
26 Part 2 of the joke
30 Flying Cloud automaker of old
31 Orange Free State settler
32 Mickey Mouse, to Donald Duck
33 It introduced a low-sugar Next version in 2012
35 Part 3 of the joke
37 Big name in Chinese-American architecture
41 Stat for Oriole hurlers
43 *Juno and the Paycock* writer O'Casey
45 Cocked item
46 Hard-shelled terrarium critter preyed on by crows
49 Amount shelled out
50 Otto ___ Bismarck
51 Queenly inits.
52 Former Eagle QB Peete
54 Part 4 of the joke
58 "Can ___ witness?"
59 End of the joke
62 So excited it shows
63 City in the shadow of Mauna Loa
64 Harding's appointee as Chief Justice
65 Infamous Scottish loch
66 Food court locale
67 Freudian studies

DOWN

1   NBA's Hawks, on scoreboards
2   When doubled, a dance
3   Spot for a crowing cock
4   Blue Jay's boo-boos, say
5   Augmented
6   Tended to the garden, in a way
7   Other, to Osvaldo
8   Square, as a debt
9   Sicilian salutation
10 Late boxing great Gatti
11 Use a keyhole, say
12 Industrial city in the Ruhr Valley
15 "Give it another shot"
17 Latin lover's word
20 Grooming sound
21 It's rolled out during a Cardinals rain delay
22 Trademarked slushy
27 "Isn't ___ bit like you . . ." (Beatles lyric)
28 *Bird* sculptor Max, 1924
29 Sapsuckers like to hang out in one
31 Cake and ice cream occasion
34 Identify hatchlings
36 Blue Hen State: Abbr.
38 Exchange of attempted calls, slangily
39 Make things smoother
40 ___-bitty
42 Fuzzy luminescence
44 Like some cleaning products
46 Shake a tail feather, say
47 Taking pills, e.g., for short
48 Sing-songy quality
49 Bank listing, briefly
50 Dove's "digital" gesture
53 Not in the coop
55 Takeoff guesses: Abbr.
56 *Eagle Eye* star LaBeouf
57 Loud shriek
60 Not a bird, not a plane sighting, to some
61 60-Down riders (if you believe in them to begin with)

Answers on page 46

ADVERB AGENCY
How do you say . . .

ACROSS

1 Airer of the popular 1983 miniseries *The Thorn Birds*
4 Rough it, say
8 Two-for-one deals, e.g., briefly
14 Mushy sentiment
15 Huge world map section
16 Colorful cousin of a carpenter?
17 "I don't give a hoot if you don't agree that I look wise," 61-Across said ___
19 Game-tying goal, i.e.
20 Evidence used to open cold cases, maybe
21 Sticks used for razing
23 Equal: Prefix
24 AL division that includes the Blue Jays
26 "Going off what you said, I think that anti-war demonstrator followed us," 61-Across ___
30 It may be lit by a rabbi
32 Drink water during a marathon, e.g.
33 Dream Team jersey letters
34 Jazzy songbird Anderson
36 Fried rice morsel
37 "Categorically speaking, that sucker just sank that putt," 61-Across ___
41 Family business?
42 Where one can talk turkey by the pound?
43 Cardinals, on the NFL Network ticker
46 Apologetic words
50 Voted into a seat
52 "Hah! You're stupid if you think that chicken is a female," 61-Across said ___
54 Bank-seized Firebird, e.g., for short
55 Ranch-suffix
56 Org. for badge-wearing Eagles
57 It acquired *Huff Post* in 2011
58 It's tested during a crisis
61 Speaker of the quotes . . . whose first and last names are bird-related
66 Lacking in energy
67 Rabbit's favorite breakfast chain?
68 Starter for -con and -classical
69 Like a can't-miss investment
70 Brings to the body shop, maybe
71 Mary's little lamb in her older years, maybe

DOWN

1 "Long ___ and Far Away"
2 Robin Hood's sporting equipment
3 Stretch of sub-zero temperatures
4 Pedro's pad
5 White Owl residue
6 "Cool" amount of money
7 Channels that come at a cost
8 Folk ballad covered by The Byrds, among many
9 Chapel rouser, for short
10 Poet's song of praise
11 Quezon City neighbor
12 Short tennis session
13 Goose-stepped, say
18 Really digging
22 Old Testament bk. after Ezra
24 Second-tallest living bird, after the ostrich
25 Divorced candidate of the 1950s, initially
26 Jazz pianist who first performed "Take Five"
27 One of six whose state bird is the northern cardinal
28 Penguin type named for an explorer's wife
29 "Dies ___ " (classic hymn)
31 Tough conditions
35 Swan song, figuratively
38 Reassuring response to "Are you hurt?"
39 Achilles' ___
40 Newspaper article heading
44 Quayle's party: Abbr.
45 Vows agreement
46 Rival of Goose and Maverick in *Top Gun*
47 Rita of *West Side Story*
48 Stocky duck (and, after you add a letter, a kid's vehicle)
49 Decade's ten: Abbr.
51 Bird invading a cornfield, often
53 Weird Al hit with the line "have some more chicken, have some more pie"
57 Dangerous slitherers
59 "No need to go into such detail" acronym
60 ___ *for Lawless* (Grafton novel)
62 "I see what your angle is"
63 Do a lawn job
64 Just a couple
65 Nail spot

Answers on page 46

ON THE JOHN J. AUDUBON MEMORIAL HIGHWAY

These things really can fly.

ACROSS

1 Hairstyle seen at Woodstock
5 Sweet-smelling wood
10 Palm Pilots, e.g.
14 One of six for a cassowary
15 Walter Braunfels' *The Birds*, for one
16 Borscht ingredient
17 Audubon Highway car #1
19 Farmland measurement
20 Cattleman's charge
21 National Park handout
23 Seoul-based make
24 Audubon Highway car #2
29 Tom, to a jake
32 They'll be seniors in two years, for short
33 ["I want my toy back!!!"]
34 Oft-debunked sky sights
36 "Well, I'll be"
37 Election season staple
40 Audubon Highway car #3
43 Sings one's praises
44 Messenger ___
45 Flock of Seagulls hit of 1982
46 1002, to Caesar
47 Words on a Wonderland confection
49 Steam room locale
50 Audubon Highway car #4
54 *Bird of Prey* actress Lesley ___ Warren
55 "We hire all sorts" abbr.
56 Snowbird's locale, often
60 Coffee shop stack
62 Audubon Highway car #5
66 Just a couple
67 What red and white cables enable, in electronics
68 Place for a plastic flamingo
69 From scratch
70 Actor's locale that has wings
71 Cardinal ___ (strict no-nos)

DOWN

1 Low cards, in cribbage
2 Uninspiring, as a performance
3 Go crazy
4 Youngster that stays up all night?
5 Rolling bed
6 Air-quality watchdog
7 "Runaway" singer ___ Shannon
8 Starbucks lurers
9 Sped towards, say
10 Sports org. whose members score turkeys
11 Perches for watching backyard birds, maybe
12 Hawk's nest
13 Acquire via the "five-finger discount"
18 Winged god of love
22 Flycatcher cousin usually found in wooded areas
25 Eastern meditation disciplines
26 Turkey is a member of it
27 Pop rockers with the 2006 hit "Over My Head"
28 Giver of Hebrew wisdom, perhaps
29 Gullible type
30 Crazy like ___
31 "Act like I'm not here"
35 Like one graceful in victory
37 Pulitzer Prize category
38 Big yapper
39 *So Big* novelist Ferber
41 Borat catchphrase
42 Like many big-city airports: Abbr.
47 Make a living, barely
48 First name among syndicated humorists
50 Model airplane wood
51 Closed shop group
52 Hassles for movers
53 Leaves the audience in stitches, as a comic
57 In vogue smoothie berry
58 Cut, like the 68-Across
59 Cozy lodgings
61 Put in stitches, as a tailor
63 Nutritionist's std.
64 Prepare to inter
65 Hawk, to a dove

Answers on page 47

MIGRATING BIRDS
Make sure these guys are in order.

ACROSS

1 Water bird #1 [Move it down]
5 Not telling the truth
10 Hasbro's Squawkers McCaw et al.
14 Crib cry
15 Water bird #2 [Keep it here]
16 ___ season (bad time to be a pheasant)
17 Site of the Taj Mahal
18 Striped mineral
19 Water bird #3 [Move it up]
20 Water bird #4 [Keep it here]
22 Snowbird Resort transport
24 Yankee nickname at the hot corner
25 Water bird #5 [Move it up]
28 Water bird #6 [Move it down]
32 "Can I have ___ of hands . . ." (quick survey)
33 Parroting types
34 Grammar mishap
36 Palindromic Dean Martin film of 1961
37 "___ Rock" (Simon and Garfunkel hit)
38 School of thought
39 Water bird #7 [Move it up]
41 Colorful bird that's Greek for "nibbling"
43 Rearward, on the USS *Kitty Hawk*
45 Starting on
46 Radio preset option, for short
47 ___ Hill (San Francisco region)
49 It may be used in building a nest
51 Narrow passageways
54 Sneaky giggle
57 Lash of old time westerns
59 With 62-Across, become organized . . . and the goal of this puzzle
60 Gear for a deep dive
62 See 59-Across
65 Wingspan or average flight speed, e.g.
66 Ode that's sung
67 Modern reading device
68 Popular computer game franchise, with "The"
69 "Who's there?" response
70 Tattoo artist's supplies

DOWN

1 Make a trade
2 Trio that followed a star
3 Bring home the bacon
4 "Oy, will this day ever end?!"
5 Large group
6 Drivers obeying triangular signs, say
7 Lovebirds' altar words
8 *Air Music* composer Rorem
9 Actresses Garbo or Gerwig
10 Smashes up, as a car
11 They're worn while watching a Verdi production
12 Pro vote
13 Show with Mr. Bill sketches
21 War-loving god
23 Foghorn Leghorn voicer Mel
25 Tom, Jake, Bill, etc.
26 Event for cowboys and clowns
27 Sneezy, Sleepy or Dopey
28 Ways to hoof it
29 Pictures featuring warped shapes, for short
30 Citrusy pie filling
31 Arizona city popular with snowbirds
35 Blender brand
38 "Are you ___ out?"
40 Clumsy cluck
42 When no turns are allowed, sometimes
44 Debris at sea
48 Panther or leopard, e.g.
50 ABA part: Abbr.
52 Forcefully ejects
53 Red Wings' stick-handling fakes
54 Great Lake that becomes a long-legged bird if you change one letter
55 67-Across download
56 Sharp-beaked predators
57 Good news for a Weight Watchers customer
58 In opposition to
61 Kid's pestering phrase, often repeated
63 Wire news serv.
64 It makes Gerald and Paul into a feminine name

Answers on page 47

TOMFOOLERY

Talkin' turkey with this one.

ACROSS

1 Capricious bird?
5 "The Nightingale and the Rose" writer Oscar
10 Supermodel Upton
14 Half of a Basque basket game
15 Swift think piece
16 Movie format for 1995's *Wings of Courage*
17 Turkey farm bartender's question?
19 Mathematical coordinates
20 Cardiologist's inserts
21 Birds that "deliver" babies, in cartoons
23 Small-of-stature Dickens character
25 Springfield shopkeeper
26 ___ country (Ryan Adams and The Cardinals genre)
27 "Honest" prez
28 Distorting effect of a turkey that's had too many Budweisers?
31 Like fishing nets
33 One who's far from a people person
34 Part of Caesar's sign-off
35 Birdbrains
37 Mr. Bill's catchphrase
41 Advance in wisdom
43 Plunge like a kestrel
44 Patriotic turkey that wants YOU!?
49 King, in Portuguese
50 Tangy beverage
51 Disgraced ex-senator Bob from Ohio
52 Fun run distance, maybe
54 Seabird with "stormy" and "gadfly" species
56 "Gosh durn it!"
57 Oil of ___
58 Like a turkey wearing its birthday suit?
62 Air Jordans maker
63 Like a kill shot
64 Preposition in the Golden Rule
65 Goes steady with
66 Suckling spots
67 Fliers grounded in 2003

DOWN

1 The Migratory Bird Treaty Act, for one
2 St. that serves as the setting for *To Kill a Mockingbird*
3 Hoarder's room
4 One pawing at birds at the window
5 Miniature hot dog
6 "Am I just crazy?"
7 WWII boats
8 Fingerpaint touch-up
9 Peacock's plumage features
10 Drug bust unit, for short
11 Without any principles
12 Bring down a Baltimore Raven, say
13 Lives and breathes
18 Move to the slow lane, as for a fast-approaching car
22 Shape of a 54-Across' nose
23 Under control
24 "Yeah right!"
25 "I've Got ___ in Kalamazoo"
29 River through Avignon
30 It's wiped often at the gym
32 Netflix competitor
35 Procedure that may aim to get rid of crow's feet, slangily
36 Landing spot in Paris
38 Lines for landscape artists
39 Ex-Oasis member Gallagher, now fronting the band High Flying Birds
40 Nickname for many a red-headed youngster
42 Feminizing suffix
43 Pintail ducks
44 Hens ideal for roasting
45 Antarctica coast noted for its penguin population
46 Do-over on a film set
47 "And your point is ...?"
48 Winged figures in much religious artwork
53 Bills of fare
55 Loaves for Reuben sandwiches
56 "___ girl!" (soccer mom's encouragement)
59 Scotchman's refusal
60 Baseball great nicknamed "Master Melvin"
61 *U.S.A.* author John ___ Passos

Answers on page 48

DOWN THE HATCH
Get your fill.

ACROSS

1 Egg on
6 Computer class at school, maybe
11 Biter in Egyptian folklore
14 The black-capped chickadee is its state bird
15 "Freedom," in Swahili
16 Raven-Symoné's label
17 Ducks like them
19 Go off, like a turkey timer
20 Breathed-in, breathed-out stuff
21 Gym rat's pride, briefly
22 "Yeah, and pigs can fly"
24 Turkeys and quails like it
26 Hummingbirds like it
29 Use a prayer rug
31 Racket or rocket extension
32 With a wide-open beak, say
33 Punch-in-the-gut response
35 Madre's hermano
37 Smidgen
38 Nuthatches and jays like it
43 Give a black eye, perhaps
44 Lip gloss container
45 Bunting head?
46 Embassy figs.
48 Pier worker's union: Abbr.
50 Defensive items for eagles
54 Orioles like it
58 Woodpeckers and tits like it
59 A Harpy eagle is on its coat of arms
60 NASA's *Eagle*, e.g.
62 *Breaking Bad* crime fighters
63 *Aces: Iron Eagle ___*
64 Theme of this puzzle
68 Paramedic's letters
69 "Billy, Don't Be ___"
70 Gut button type?
71 Potsdam pronoun
72 Red ___ (playground game)
73 Got smart, with "up"

DOWN

1 Words upon a return
2 Crane of *Psycho*
3 Second-smallest state capital, by population
4 Alfonso XIII's queen
5 Swan lover of myth
6 Go on a wild goose chase, say
7 Steven in the Obama cabinet
8 Abner's radio partner
9 Shady garden area
10 "Poppycock!"
11 Remove a leg, perhaps
12 Rummy 500 need
13 Dismissed quickly, with "over"
18 *Falcon Crest* airer
23 Union that merged with AFTRA in 2012
25 Like some Crayola colors
27 Hallmark card category
28 Songbird India___
30 Upstairs apartment
34 Avian ___
36 Spherical object
38 *Spider-Man* director, 2002
39 One living in a high-rise, likely
40 Theatrical honor a step down from a Tony
41 Brief period of time?
42 They carry a shock in the water
43 Animated birds Heckle and Jeckle, for two
47 Relaxing retreat
49 Totally sold on, as an idea
51 IRS man's procedures
52 It's cased on the grill, slangily
53 Produced a show on Broadway
55 Throw in the clink
56 Oscar-winning song from *Slumdog Millionaire*
57 "___ haw!"
61 Catty remark?
65 Flock leader, for short
66 Hip hop Dr.
67 Serious traffic offense

Answers on page 46

I MOLT WITH YOU
We're dealing with a light subject here.

ACROSS

1 Far from upbeat
5 Small dust-up
10 Polish *Good Bird* articles, say
14 Cartoonist Peter
15 "One of ___ Nights" (Eagles hit)
16 Aviation-related prefix
17 Feature of risqué comedy
18 *Achievement to be proud of, idiomatically
20 Stat larger for flightless birds than flying birds, as a rule
22 Give one the latest details
23 Stick in a boathouse
24 It's "positive" in Paris
26 "...Cyprus black as ___ was crow" (Shakespeare)
27 Many an exec's holding
30 *Nickname of Army general Winfield Scott
33 Hotel room staple
34 Try out, as a pickup line
35 Cheese used in a Greek pastry known as tiropita
36 Molts, like the answers to the starred clues
41 Improve one's skills
42 Mideast prince: Var.
43 Long-extinct cousin of the ostrich
44 *Publicly humiliated, in a way
50 Turn-___
51 Global workers gp.
52 It may shoot birds without harming them, for short
53 Feel terrible about
54 Mid-flight connection
57 Waiting to ride a roller coaster, say
59 *Dance, slangily
62 Future "*avis*"
63 One of many in a French door
64 Ivan dominant on clay
65 Songbird Winans
66 Lady Bird Johnson's middle name
67 "No kidding!"
68 Preferred way to watch football on TV, for many

DOWN

1 Korean automaker discontinued in 2011
2 It's no walk in the park
3 Loosen a belt
4 *Walkabout* director Nicolas
5 Facebook postings, e.g.
6 X, on frats
7 Saline solution brand
8 Major won by Kite and Goosen
9 Repaired
10 Cardinal point (not in a bird sense)
11 Month with high electric bills, for many
12 Nest egg that "hatches" upon retirement
13 Whirligig
19 Wings for Dumbo
21 Word with bird or hen
25 "Time ___ the essence!"
28 Dog track actions
29 Wisdom-extracting org.?
31 Circuit breaker predecessor
32 Have ___ miss (barely avoid)
35 Bird's nest ___ (flowerless plant)
36 Water bird also known as a diver
37 Not level
38 City in the center of the Hawkeye State
39 All-Star lefty for the Blue Jays in 2004
40 Chick who called Lakers games
41 Gp. with copays
44 Fork part
45 Basic stuff in chemistry?
46 Beaten badly
47 Highly motivated
48 Harem guard
49 Formed an opinion
55 Furniture giant headquartered in Europe
56 Says a play is a turkey, say
58 Centers in geometry
59 Hot tub
60 Holbrook of *Jonathan Livingston Seagull*
61 Muckraker Tarbell

Answers on page 47

CAW ME MAYBE
Do you have my number?

ACROSS

1 Mocking laughter
5 Wave pom-poms for the Cardinals, perhaps
10 Court legend Arthur
14 Death notice, briefly
15 Chuck
16 Give a good slap
17 Org. against duck hunting
18 Hatch in Washington
19 ___ Sad (second-largest Serbian city)
20 Super-popular magic tricks, e.g.
23 Tail feather, slangily
25 York or Pepper's rank: Abbr.
26 Triple ___ (orange liqueur)
27 Segment that lacks sides
28 Go like the Road Runner
31 Ambulance fig.
33 Prized all-white flower
36 Like the Orioles, while wearing gray
40 Quick summary
41 One keeping a nest egg?
42 Obeyed the rooster's call
43 Sets a price
44 Flock of doves?
46 "The Raven" writer
48 Beauty queen's article
49 One of two in "cuckoo"
50 Justice Dept. arm
53 Boxer who said "It's a job. Grass grows, birds fly, waves pound the sand. I beat people up."
55 Ones schlepping
57 "Mr. Jones" band, and what you're doing after completing this puzzle
61 Makes a boo-boo
62 "Canary Yellow" boat in a Gordon Lightfoot song
63 When high fliers are due in, briefly
66 "Time ___ the essence!"
67 Jim Croce's "I Got ___"
68 Homeowner's option, briefly
69 Lillehammer's land: Abbr.
70 Unfamiliar with
71 ___ fixe

DOWN

1 Move to another lily pad, say
2 Lincoln who had a pet turkey
3 The Birds director with a bird in his name
4 Gaming platform for Road Runner
5 Thick creamy soup
6 Group of wrens or cranes
7 Wyatt of the wild west
8 Pandora's box contents
9 Weaseled out of a commitment
10 Grainy bristles
11 Wingtips, e.g.
12 Le ___ (French port city)
13 FDR's denomination: Abbr.
21 Ahead
22 Bank drive-thru box
23 Major Iraq city
24 European sea eagles
29 Have a sore hammy, say
30 Birds whose name roughly means "ground," fittingly
32 Poi source
34 Bee-eater's treat
35 Ancient Peruvian
37 Holy Cross locale
38 According to
39 They're positive
42 Flu sufferer's sound
44 It's got a big bill and floats
45 Thoroughfare for The Boss
47 Granola goodie
50 ___ the hole (secret asset)
51 Above-the-waist area
52 High anger
54 Cockamamie
56 Ear-flicking kid, say
58 [Don't click on this link on the job]
59 Enjoy a chew toy
60 Unresponsive state
64 Top-100 movies list org.
65 Total one gets after 57-Across, using the completed grid word-search style

Answers on page 46

REACH FOR THE SKY
Creating a flap with this one.

ACROSS

1 Big explosion creator, for short
6 Angry herds?
10 Way out there
14 Turkey region, in ancient times
15 Follow the rules
16 Eastern guru
17 Performs, biblically
18 Cabbie's derisive comment to a kiwi?
20 The Yardbirds' homeland: Abbr.
21 Ones making droll comments, say
23 "Blame it on the Bossa Nova" warbler Eydie
24 Acrophobic excuse cited by an emu?
28 *Batman & Robin* star Thurman
29 Soccer legend Hamm
30 Org. involved in the Janet Jackson "wardrobe malfunction" scandal
33 Jimmy declared dead in 1982
36 Daffy Duck, for one
38 Carson succeeded him
39 "Sentence" served by a naughty ostrich?
42 Hence
43 Ocean spot for petrels, perhaps
44 ___ grebe (water bird with showy neck feathers)
45 Hor. counterpart
46 "Stop," from Martin Scorsese
47 Tool similar to an ax
48 Caprice thought up by a rhea?
55 "The Birds of Prey" writer T. S.
57 Ancient people that worshiped condors
58 Prior to, in verse
59 Sanctuary holding cassowaries?
62 Perry Mason's workload
64 Not just regional: Abbr.
65 Swenson of *Benson*
66 Lauder who said "Beauty is an attitude"
67 Old Tunisian bigwigs
68 37-Down, for one
69 Box set array

DOWN

1 Sharper-image TV option, briefly
2 Crooner Pat with trademark white shoes
3 Massive Russian lake
4 Grafton's ___ *for Malice*
5 DC comics gliding gal
6 March or May, e.g.
7 Like an overly plump chicken
8 Insect feasted on by many passerines
9 Pink Floyd founder Barrett
10 Distribute, as funds
11 "Them's the rules"
12 Radio button
13 Give an assessment
19 Turkish title of old
22 "___ tree falls in the forest . . ."
25 "April Fools" singer Wainwright
26 "Later, alligator"
27 Vannelli of disco fame
31 Sidewalk eatery
32 Street ___ (thug's reputation)
33 *Disaster DIY* airer
34 "Do not add to his words, ___ will rebuke you . . ." (Proverbs)
35 Ten to five
36 Eagles don't have any
37 Keats' "___ to a Nightingale"
38 Fountain site
40 It can be a downer
41 Like an "embarrassed" cormorant?
46 Phoenix, for one
47 Baltimore Ravens' org.
49 Kills time lazily
50 Splash of color
51 Night owl's time, maybe
52 Spots for breeding and incubation
53 Shallow river
54 Flunky's frequent responses
55 It's northwest of Stillwater
56 Singular
60 Secure a sweater, perhaps
61 Lennon wrote "Woman" for her
63 "___ was saying . . ."

Answers on page 47

DIGITAL DISPLAY

Just showing who's number one.

ACROSS

1 *Falling Skies* channel
4 Miss a birdie but avoid a bogey, say
11 Wells Fargo holdings: Abbr.
16 Jim Palmer, for the Orioles
17 Words on the back of a ten-cent piece
18 Hang limply
19 Big South Conference member from North Carolina
21 Slangy word said with a shrug
22 Pago Pago is there
23 Gadgets for golfers
25 Cement-making direction
26 Builder who may suggest solar power
31 Radical gp. of the 1970s
34 Onetime flier with the slogan "Up, Up, and Away"
35 Suffix meaning "word"
36 *Murphy Brown* title portrayer
42 iPhone, for one
45 "That a fact?"
46 Him, to Henri
47 Big name in bubbly
48 Cabinet position until 1971
53 "___ tu" (1974 hit for Mocedades)
54 Popular Saturn model
55 "Not today, amigo"
56 Migrating month for many birds: Abbr.
57 1992 sequel featuring The Penguin
61 NBA All-Star Lamar
63 Otto's "one"
64 Sun ___-sen
65 Absolut offering reminiscent of Hawaii
72 Figures in *The Sting*?
73 Bird lover John who founded the Sierra Club
74 Zac of *The Paperboy*
78 Patty Hearst's alias in the 31-Across
80 Make a contemptuous gesture, slangily . . . and a hint to solving this puzzle's long answers
84 McCullough's *The ___ Birds*
85 Splinter group
86 Chick tail?
87 Spread one's seeds
88 Like an irregular triangle
89 Just swell

DOWN

1 Facebook photo identifiers
2 Org. for the Jayhawks and Golden Eagles
3 Jailbird's stint
4 Angler's aid
5 *Wheel of Fortune* buy
6 What the V stands for on a Bible's spine: Abbr.
7 One of eight Brit. kings
8 Michelangelo chipped away at it for almost two years
9 Honey's hue
10 Pear-shaped fiddle
11 Count the beans
12 Having a sour attitude, slangily
13 One who's about the same age
14 Barkeep's mixer
15 Clay pigeon shooting, for one
20 Kennel pet
24 Title purple martin of the funnies pages
27 ___-Sketch
28 Ram's mate
29 Catch a crook
30 Lovebirds' getaway
31 Did some recon, with "out"
32 Major Punjab city
33 "It should be just a matter of time"
37 Case workers: Abbr.
38 "___ the Walrus"
39 Barack's second Supreme Court nominee
40 Capek play of 1922
41 Show for The Eagles
43 *Star Trek* counselor Troi
44 After a long wait
47 Posting at Popeye's
49 Warm an egg, say
50 The turkey with the beard
51 Make changes to a law
52 Bryce Harper, e.g., briefly
57 Feathered wrap
58 Toggle on a clock radio
59 Harry Reid's st.
60 2010 animated film featuring macaws and toucans
62 Have an itch
65 Annie of *Ghostbusters*
66 State with a panhandle
67 Cocoa ___ (cereal pitched by Sonny the Cuckoo Bird)
68 Shade similar to lavender
69 Vamp of soap-opera fame
70 Seat of New Hampshire's Cheshire County
71 Some fliers' home: Abbr.
75 *Live! With Kelly* host
76 Popular Blizzard flavor
77 St. with a 2010s oil boom
79 "The Owl ___ the Pussycat"
81 Former TV ministry letters
82 Ravens rarity
83 Turtledove

Answers on page 46

GAME BIRDS
Play along with me here.

ACROSS

1. Bird sent out by Noah after the great flood
5. Seaman's patron
11. 1860s alliance, briefly
14. Et ___ (and others)
15. Tobacco brand with a bear logo
16. Part of a bird cage?
17. *Eagle known for defensive tactics
19. Vows words
20. Adjust a corset, perhaps
21. Radicals fight it
23. Highlanders
24. *Hawk known for exceptional vertical ability despite small stature
26. WWII premier Tojo
29. Propeller down the river
30. Flying heroes
33. "Lady" prog-rockers
34. Butcher's tool
37. Seahawk's divisional foe
38. What each of the answers to the starred clues is
40. www.audubon.___
41. Dennis who George Costanza modeled his haircut after in *Seinfeld*
43. Lioness in *The Lion King*
44. Fly in the ointment
45. Modern, in Munich
46. Gov't worker doing audits, perhaps
48. *Cardinal known for superior speed
51. Working in tandem
55. Title role for Denis Leary in 1994
56. Oklahoma tribe whose flag features a 22-Down
58. Chick
59. *Penguin known for having many points on the ice
62. "…man ___ mouse?"
63. Striped birthstones
64. One in the hole
65. Ruffle one's feathers
66. Positive votes: Var.
67. Group of quails

DOWN

1. Flies like a hummingbird
2. Acid used in soaps
3. *The Road* star Mortensen
4. Many pizza slices, fractionally speaking
5. ___-Ball (arcade game)
6. Mayors run it
7. Old Norse letter (hidden in RED HEN)
8. 52, to Caesar
9. South China Sea island
10. "No problem-o!"
11. Benchmark of analysis
12. Wax bottom?
13. Mushroom cloud maker, for short
18. Formal reply to "Who's there?"
22. Bird that's full of grace
24. Passerine known as an "alouette" in Canada
25. TV screen makeup
27. "Spring ahead" hrs.
28. Relating to cultural groups
30. Bird dog's [I found the scent!]
31. Thunderbird, e.g.
32. Frequent collaborator with Yo-Yo Ma
35. Monk's title
36. Hatchling-to-be
38. Blue-colored songbird native to South America
39. Cap worn by 23-Across
42. Southern neighbor of S. Dak.
44. Scam executed with excessive flattery
47. Not quite closed
48. State's second-in-command, briefly
49. Take-off spot in Chicago
50. Old enough
52. Simply stunned
53. Arid part of Israel
54. Football analyst Bradshaw
56. Captain Hook's baddie
57. Unhappy cockatiel's sound
60. Dorm leaders, briefly
61. Tie-breaking periods, for short

Answers on page 47

SEAL THE DEAL
This puzzle is quite the stretch.

ACROSS

1   More-popular wax half, usually
6   Sound from a nest
11 Toy that you can take for a spin
14 Mister, in Monterrey
15 Hoffman's *Outbreak* co-star
16 Horton heard one
17 Title Ibsen newlywed
19 Fried chicken need
20 Label for Doves
21 "Absolutely!"
22 Guiding principles
24 They intensify in a library
29 Heart scan letters
30 Catholic school subj.
31 See 60-Down
33 Loony bins, e.g.
36 Strange ___ circumstances (tough spot)
38 ___ *Boot* (1981 submarine film)
39 Like a bad liar, say
42 Some intro-course instructors, for short
43 Girl in a Beethoven title
44 The "Bird-Language" poet W. H.
45 First computer-animated film to be released on DVD
47 Outdoorsy prefix
48 Birdbrain
49 Elizabeth Swann portrayer in the *Pirates of the Caribbean* series
55 Song likely not featured on *Glee*
56 I. M. who designed a wing of Boston's Museum of Fine Arts
57 Inventor Whitney, or what he was as a collegian
58 Massive set for a lexicographer
59 Avian symbol on the Great Seal . . . or an explanation of this puzzle's theme
64 Airport heavies since 2002: Abbr.
65 Current fashion
66 Shelled creeper
67 Messy digs, to a mom
68 Soft drinks that can give you a buzz
69 Like some kitchen floors

DOWN

1   Peter of Peter and Gordon
2   Haunting words from a boss
3   Where the Jerdon's courser was spotted in 1986, ending speculation it was extinct
4   Pentagon div.
5   Wipe out completely
6   Bond portrayer in *Skyfall*
7   Where many fliers converge
8   Bilingual class, for short
9   Phoenix-to-Dallas dir.
10 Things opened in a sauna?
11 Like the bird on Albania's flag
12 The Buckeyes of the Big Ten
13 They run for seats, briefly
18 Bell hit with a hammer
23 *Dungeons & Dragons* co.
25 Crème ___ crème
26 Richard once married to Natalie Wood
27 Don't bother anymore
28 Ex-Cardinal Matty
32 The A of NBA: Abbr.
33 Terrier of '30s cinema
34 Like the most expensive hotel suite, say
35 Beatles song covered over 2,200 times
36 ___ and snee
37 Least under the radar
40 Intestinal sections (found in MILEAGE)
41 The hots
46 Hummingbird movement
48 Like Wild Turkey
50 Sits on a perch
51 Modern platforms to read *Bird Watcher's Digest*
52 Like in-season hunting
53 She deeded Southfork to Bobby Ewing
54 On-ramp sign
55 Candy similar to Crows
60 With 31-Across, in proportion
61 Scarlet tanager's color
62 Bambi's aunt
63 Black cuckoo

Answers on page 47

31

SCHOOL SPIRIT
Featuring some class-y birds.

ACROSS

1 East Lansing sch.
4 Email heading
8 "Well, if you say so . . ."
14 Noise violation responders, briefly
15 "Gotta fly," to Federico
16 Distinctive markings on some ducks
17 Delaware athletes
19 Reminiscent of "The Raven," for instance
20 *Twins* director Reitman
21 Waits on hand and foot
23 Fitting
24 Southern Mississippi athletes
28 Shrimp in a butter and garlic sauce
29 Leg of the *Casablanca* love triangle
33 Brewery monstrosity
36 Pre-CIA spy org.
37 Bowling Green athletes
40 Having gained lumps, as milk
42 Withstand heckling, say
43 North Florida athletes
45 Gas additive brand
46 Battle of Seattle gp.
47 Literally, Spanish for "weight"
48 Plays the peeping Tom
51 Coastal Carolina athletes
57 Palindromic Nabokov novel
60 Words of compassion
61 Field of expertise
62 Desert known for Joshua trees
64 Youngstown State athletes
67 Shrub poisonous to many birds
68 Nate Archibald's alma mater
69 French pronoun
70 Gender discrimination
71 Low-ranking mil. members
72 "Whassup?"

DOWN

1 Nickname for a boss
2 Simultaneous gunfire, in the military
3 Par for the course
4 Goethe's groan
5 Rare result for the Seahawks
6 Bikes built for two
7 "Outta luck," in old slang (or a lack of Dove?)
8 Light a fire under
9 Flier from Canada, often
10 Native engaged in the Black Hawk War
11 "Tell Mama" warbler James
12 Small transgression
13 They break off from the flock
18 Ones who may be tight for the Ravens?
22 "Don't have to worry about work for two days" initialism
25 Learning place, in Lyon
26 Treacherous, as weather
27 Awesome, in modern slang
30 Big name in movie theaters
31 Ruffled-feathers behavior
32 Regarding, on memos
33 1976 Herbie Hancock album reminiscent of cognac
34 Sacred domed room
35 Outfit halves
38 Room under a rooftop
39 Flap on a blazer
41 ___ Z (Camaro model)
44 Ducks' opponent in the 2007 NHL Finals, briefly
45 *Pros vs. Joes* cable airer
49 Cork, as a wine bottle
50 Chargers great Junior
52 Bee-eaters may wait near them to attack prey
53 Squad above the scrubs
54 Romance novelist Segal
55 Jude and Nicole's *Cold Mountain* co-star
56 With a fresh attitude
57 Latin lover's word?
58 Be a bad night watchman
59 Bathtub cleanser brand
63 Clay, after 1964
65 Brooklyn hoopster
66 TomTom unit, e.g.

Answers on page 47

FLIGHT PATTERN

These guys sure rack up the frequent flier miles.

ACROSS

1 Rooster on the roof?
5 Taper off
10 Czech mate?
14 Shape of an egg
15 *Oedipus the King* character
16 Rikki-tikki-___ (fictional mongoose)
17 It may move a loon
18 Cardinal's head?
19 Word on French restaurant menus
20 8, in Roman numerals
22 Norway's patron saint
24 Sarcastic reply to an emotional plea
27 Builds a nest egg, say
31 Cosmonaut Alexey, the first to walk in space
32 It "gets the red out," per its ads
33 Chick ___
34 Brings back into popularity
38 Body scan org.
39 Beekman Tower architect Frank
41 Gabor or Green
42 *El Condor,* for one
44 Creme-filled cookie
45 Figure skating coups
47 Phoebe or Polly, perhaps
48 Political cartoonist Ted
50 Arctic Circle bird
52 Use a V-formation, (which is visually depicted in this puzzle's grid)
55 Using a V-formation can combat it
58 Sean Lennon's middle name
59 Many birds do it in the winter
61 Modern trial evidence
62 Instrument that symbolizes the duck in *Peter and the Wolf*
64 Hailstorm portrayer in *Scary Movie*
65 Ex-Oriole Aparicio
66 Needing directions, say
67 They're off limits
68 Entr'___
69 Tomahawks, hatchets, e.g.
70 Towards the left, at sea
71 Docket of events, slangily

DOWN

1 Sacred words
2 Gardner of *The Blue Bird*
3 USNA part: Abbr.
4 Flap on a wing
5 Meet a goal
6 Cornrows segment
7 ___ Lingus
8 Big commotions
9 Country completely within another country
10 Holds (off), as an invasion
11 School head, for short?
12 St. crosser
13 Crooner Damone
21 Dove competitor
23 Dispatch boat
24 Volunteer's offer
25 ___ & Frank (longtime department store chain)
26 Bird of nursery rhymes
28 He's no safe quacker?
29 Al of racing fame
30 Bead from an oyster
35 Confuse to no end
36 "___ Gotta Crow" (*Peter Pan* song)
37 Kilmer of *Wings of Courage*
40 Lionize?
43 Prefix big in the farming business
45 Central Pennsylvania city
46 Opponent of laissez-faire policies
49 Fall behind
51 Biblical verb ending
52 Money, slangily
53 Where to receive postage-free mail
54 Bar, to a barrister
55 Public outrage
56 Dovetail together
57 Lightened one's load, perhaps
60 Wine snob's prefix
63 Fliers of UFOs
65 ___ Palmas (Canary Islands hotspot)

Answers on page 46

CAMPAIGN TO RE-ELECT SENATOR BIRD
It's looking like a tough road ahead.

ACROSS

1 It's needed for a long migration
8 551, to Ovid
11 Airspeed ratio
15 They're real downers
16 McKellen who performed *The Seagull* on the stage in 2007
17 Hand lotion soother
18 Because of his militant leanings, Senator Bird was labeled by his opponent as a ___
19 Blood cell element, briefly
21 Building manager, for short
22 Morsel for an oriole
24 Rapper's accompaniments
25 Tattoo spot
27 Started the hibachi
29 Young '___ (brood)
31 Instead of rehearsing his speech for the rally, Senator Bird ___
33 Ice Cube hairstyle, slangily
36 "Can't help you, pal"
38 Hole in a bird's head
39 Brief pants?
40 In the debate, Senator Bird denied accusations that he ___ by using power for financial gain
44 Some Stanford grads: Abbr.
45 Playing hard to get
46 Twelve-volume Trojan epic
47 Ike's monogram
48 After being defeated in the election, Senator Bird served the rest of his term as a ___
51 Winter precip., in many ads
52 Mexican peninsula that's home to many flamingos
53 Antonym: Abbr.
55 Tebowing joints
58 Beaks: Var.
59 Radames' girl in opera
62 Some lanyard attachments
64 On his final day in office, Senator Bird ___ and admitted to prior wrongdoing
67 Weight on one's back
68 Auction offering
69 Good for farming, as soil
70 Clean one's Skylark
71 *Angry Birds* between-level annoyances
72 Lived and breathed

DOWN

1 Pen mothers
2 "Heart and Soul" hitmakers, 1987
3 Part of a duct system
4 Bill of political humor
5 "Consider ___ blessing"
6 ___ World oriole
7 Invites for coffee, say
8 Hole that must be filled
9 Over-the-top genteel
10 Like Beethoven's Sixth
11 Fended off a would-be attacker, in a way
12 Ski resort near Snowbird, Utah
13 "Bald" water bird
14 Bath towel embroidery
20 Act as the look-out man, perhaps
23 Hen's laying
26 Big peck sound?
28 Romanian tennis star Ion, nicknamed "Count Dracula"
29 Peckish
30 Seemingly forever
32 Herb that'll make you gag
33 One who marches to one's own beat
34 Contents of a pitching mound bag
35 Perform better than
37 Tense times for Falcons fans
39 Former C & W channel
41 Juno or Janus, e.g.
42 "Read the smallest row you can" exams
43 Former Zaire president Mobuto Sese ___
48 Strong desire
49 Small amount of shampoo
50 Not child-proofed, say
52 "Well, I'll be"
54 Post-war signings
55 "Do I ___ you from somewhere?"
56 Doting oldster's nickname
57 Fast-running Down Under birds
60 Bush staved him off in 1988
61 Really impressed
63 Atticus Finch's home st.
65 Daffy Duck creator Avery
66 "___ tu" (Verdi aria)

Answers on page 46

LISPOMANIA
Celebrating quite the animated character.

ACROSS

1 Bring into the fold
5 80, for Grey Goose
10 First book after the Gospels
14 The A of UAE
15 John Hancock rival in the insurance game
16 Chicken's dwelling
17 *Charge to use tires on the highway?
19 It's big in Japan, in two ways
20 Modern TV option
21 Celeste of *Chicken Every Sunday*, 1949
23 Flying Cloud automaker of old
24 So far
25 Tina's ex-hubby
27 *Emulate a Wild West sheriff?
29 Prominent feature of a cockatiel
31 *"JAG"* spin-off
32 Green gem
35 Where David Cameron prepped
37 Ragweed reaction, for many
40 "Tan"?
43 Zellweger with an Oscar
44 Big name in college grants
45 It holds tunes for a jogger
46 Soft mineral
48 Thaw wings before flight
50 *Skin pic of the underworld?
53 Nipper's company
54 Leathernecks' entertainment gp.
57 Tide competitor
58 Perched on the highest branch, say
60 Did a laundry chore
62 Ear-splitting
64 Notable canary whose speech impediment is used on the answers to the starred clues
66 Do a lawn chore
67 Take flight
68 Sermon or kitchen add-on
69 Oldish fruit-flavored soda brand
70 Made a transgression
71 ___ of the Rooster (Chinese zodiac period)

DOWN

1 Bird-woman of Greek mythology
2 Not-so-modest comment after a win
3 West African metropolis
4 Flows' opposites
5 Flier known as a "budgie" in Australia
6 Emeritus: Abbr.
7 "That being said . . . ," to a texter
8 At the minimum setting, as a hot plate
9 Like disgraced angels
10 Summertime needs, briefly
11 Period of pitching woo
12 Marisa ironically nominated for a Razzie for *Oscar*
13 Shape of some water bird's bills
18 14-Across royal
22 Colorful South American bird that talks
26 Prevent, in legalese
28 Ross's duet partner on "Endless Love"
29 Product hawked by Sonny the Cuckoo Bird or Cornelius the Rooster
30 Lugged
32 Vlasic container
33 State of amazement
34 Lead-in to an embarrassing story, perhaps
36 Penguin or Red Wing, for short
38 Platte River native

39 Ref. work that added "retweet" to its twelfth edition
41 Flier based in Atlanta
42 Drew out
47 Stampede group
49 *Father Goose* star ___ Grant
50 "I Am Woman" singer Reddy
51 Give in to water or wind, like a beach
52 Urban skyline feature
54 Bring together
55 Feather mattress pad maker
56 More duck-y?
59 ". . . and a partridge in a ___ tree"
61 Follow instructions
63 Latin God
65 Genesis gal

Answers on page 47

POWER POSITION

Get a charge out of this one.

ACROSS

1 Emus lay green ones
5 Spaghetti sauce herb
10 Tweety Bird didn't know his
13 Having a suspicious attitude (about)
14 Flared dress style
15 Many a magazine article title
16 Wine-making brother of Julio
18 Layer of paper or wood
19 Means of telephonic espionage
20 Lacking creativity, say
22 Bug spray ingredient
23 Kid on a sugar rush, for one
25 Gives a coy smile
27 Like an eagle showing its wingspan
30 "___ we there yet?"
33 Fat adored by woodpeckers
34 "Rapture" singer Baker
35 Scrubbers by the kitchen sink
37 Root used in some herbal medicines
39 Girl with loose morals
40 Wingdings, for one
41 Flier to Oslo
42 Shout accompanied by a fist pump, perhaps
43 Like the Japanese cormorant
46 1960s Giants quarterback nicknamed "Bald Eagle"
48 California setting for *Easy A*
52 2002–08 HBO police drama
54 Game to which 46-Across was selected seven times
56 Harrison of *The Honey Pot*
57 1990 Mel Gibson movie, which is visually demonstrated four times in this puzzle
59 Constellation that neighbors Scorpio
60 Laura of *ER*
61 Body with many members of the *parti socialiste*
62 It helps prevent sticking
63 One who may speak for Cardinals and Falcons
64 Cough syrup meas.

DOWN

1 Like urban legends
2 Horror or comedy, e.g.
3 Gives a handshake, maybe
4 GPS part: Abbr.
5 Scotch instrument with a drone and a chanter
6 Chicken ___ king
7 Metallic color of a Thunderbird, perhaps
8 Headache around the holidays, for some
9 Téa who starred in *Flying Blind*
10 All-American treats
11 Tern relative
12 One-named singer who declined the chance to score *Titanic*
13 Not for youngsters
17 6000-page epic in Aramaic and Hebrew
21 Short game sticks
24 Doc examining Polly, say
26 Brit's quaint oath
28 Peak where Typhon was defeated, in myth
29 Carps to no end
30 Like a messy hearth
31 Amoral womanizer
32 English comp. final, perhaps
34 Start to freeze?
36 "Yeah, and emus can fly!"
37 Hockey net's metallic edge
38 Unpaid helper, maybe
40 In great shape
43 Letting out, as one's grievances
44 *Tristram Shandy* author Laurence
45 Halloween decoration
47 Long bone for a stilt
49 Gets an Audubon Society membership, e.g.
50 "That's ___!" (director's cry)
51 "Would ___ you down?"
52 It might be baited to attract turkeys
53 Zeus' wife
55 Hops are dried there
58 Couch potato's favorite room

Answers on page 47

BYRDS COVER SONGS
Getting a little punny here.

ACROSS

1 Betray embarrassment
6 Office-wide email, say
10 Ex-Oriole slugger Sammy
14 Noted Soviet novelist Yuri
15 Thickener used in some Japanese dishes
16 Pass over, as for a nomination
17 The Byrds' cover of a 1991 Extreme ballad?
19 Splitsville, Nevada
20 Place for traveling lovebirds
21 1921–23 presidential monogram
22 Clown shoe specs
24 www.phoenix.___
25 The Byrds' cover of a 1965 Supremes hit?
30 Paquin of *Fly Away Home*
31 Francophone's class, maybe
32 Beat by a run, perhaps
33 The Byrds' cover of a jazzy 1970 Van Morrison hit?
37 He played Bob in *La Bamba*
39 Chalks it up (to)
40 The Byrds' cover of a 1993 #1 hit off the *Three Musketeers* soundtrack?
45 "... but for the grace of God ___"
46 Not much longer
49 Very small, slangily
50 Mohawk need
51 The Byrds' cover of a 1978 Gloria Gaynor disco hit?
54 Causes the boo birds to come alive, say
55 Woodwind used in the *Swan Lake* theme
56 The Byrds' cover of a 1976 Barbra Streisand hit?
60 "As a conclusion ..."
63 The Engineers of the ECAC
65 Penlight batteries
66 The Byrds' cover of a 1986 Bangles hit?
72 Defunct telecom giant
73 It often departs airports but lacks wings
74 Jan. honoree
75 Screenwriter Vardalos
76 Wintertime conveyance
78 The Byrds' cover of, er ... well, their own 1965 hit
82 Flying start?
83 "... ___ saw Elba"
84 They "scrape" the sky
85 Drizzle
86 Benchmarks: Abbr.
87 Meager

DOWN

1 Mel who voiced Daffy Duck and Tweety
2 Give the OK
3 Direct Cardinal fans to their seats, say
4 One-named rapper who is Buddy Guy's daughter
5 Game where arms and legs aren't wanted
6 Red China name
7 White-tailed wading birds
8 Used the turn lane, maybe
9 Figure skater Brian
10 Lithuania, once: Abbr.
11 Robin's daily lay
12 Dessert option at Red Robin
13 Teem
14 Chaplin's bride
17 Sci-fi/comedy franchise with a 2012 sequel, on posters
18 Five-year-old's question, often
23 Like unset makeup
26 Jayhawker's state: Abbr.
27 Not Rep. or Dem.
28 Banana throwaway
29 Terse confession
33 The Twitter bird, e.g.
34 "That really hurts!"
35 Parisienne's peeper
36 "Do you mind?"
38 Maritime distress signal
41 Schreiber of *Taking Woodstock*
42 Storybook hulk
43 "Swallow" can be used as one, but not "sparrow"
44 As an alternative
46 Hand in
47 Start of Montana's motto
48 Apply too much pressure
52 Gospel music subgenre
53 Blood line
54 "Step the meek fowls where ___ they ranged": Emerson
57 Aerie newborns
58 Longtime McDonald's magnate
59 Empty space
60 2001 Sean Penn film featuring Beatles covers
61 Centers of cells
62 Snowbird resort customers
64 Like the birds on Noah's ark
67 Middleton and Moss
68 Crisis responder, for short
69 Nonreactive, like some gases
70 Runs *Wings* reruns, e.g.
71 One of the Bobbsey Twins
77 One of six in 38-Down, in Morse
79 Start of Sue Grafton's fourteenth book in a popular series
80 Pioneering gangsta rap group
81 Bill featuring Hamilton

Answers on page 46

THIS BIRD'S FOR HUE

Featuring some "shady" avian descriptors.

ACROSS

1 Bill seen after eating and drinking
4 Freak out, slangily
9 Dash on a calculator
14 A bald eagle evokes it, often
15 Held the deed for
16 Left one's perch, say
17 Advanced degree in filmmaking, perhaps
18 Dress cut that widens at the hem
19 Title Seuss character in a 2012 hit film
20 Excessively descriptive author Amis?
23 *The West Wing* Emmy winner Alan
24 Business card no.
25 Followed one's rules
29 They're fragile in Hollywood
31 Down-in-the-dumps host Leno?
32 Like some jeans or memories
34 Chicken salad ingredient
36 Maker of the Genesis console
37 Syst. where "bird" is touching your forefinger to your thumb over your mouth.
38 Clear as day
41 Proofing letters in math class
42 Aoki of the Champions Tour
44 Potato ___ (Taco Johns side)
45 They're "earned" by cowpokes
47 Visibly irate skateboarder Tony?
49 Aaron Spelling's eldest
50 Practice stingy defense
51 White-crested things: Abbr.
53 Tablet for playing *Angry Birds*, perhaps
56 Far from courageous detective Mike?
59 Kutcher's *Killers* co-star
62 Brought home KFC, say
63 Mark "The Bird" Fidrych led the league in it in 1976
64 Sing one's praises
65 Strict and severe
66 Peace or beat ending
67 Shirk, as one's duties
68 Sidekick for the Lone Ranger
69 It might break as a result of a swing

DOWN

1 It neighbors St. Pete
2 Far from brilliant
3 "Hairy" carnival attraction
4 Coup for the Penguins
5 Parliament members that may have been born yesterday?
6 Far east cartoon genre
7 Relating to jailbirds
8 River through central Germany (anagram of DEER)
9 Its police chief described it as a "nice, quiet beach community" in *The Big Lebowski*
10 Literary twists
11 Neither fish ___ fowl
12 Airer of the '90s cartoon *Duckman*
13 Reason for an TV-MA rating
21 One of many in *The Pelican Brief*
22 Picker-upper for a condor
26 Turntables, headphones, amps, etc.
27 Hot to trot, so to speak
28 Pairings
30 "___ to a Nightingale"
31 Off weeks, for football teams
32 Where ducks and chickens get ribbons
33 Good ledger entry
34 It "does a body good"
35 Fruity roadside offering
39 Swifts and storks have one each
40 General at many a Chinese buffet
43 [Gasp]
46 Wearing a tight corset, say
48 *Moonstruck* actor Danny
49 Gift shop purchase
51 "Aim High . . . Fly-Fight-Win," for the U.S. Air Force
52 Carly Rae Jepsen fan, likely
54 Falcon's nest
55 Male mallard
57 Like a "rotten egg"
58 ___ Domini
59 Female mallard
60 Outer: Prefix
61 Cousin of '60s TV

Answers on page 48

RIGHT BACK AT YA
Do I hear an echo?

ACROSS

1 Calling a 16-Across a bird, say
5 Cardinal's footwear
10 Bad night to get a zit
14 Robin's ursine friend
15 "Stormy Weather" warbler Lena
16 Titled woman
17 ___ de Lobos (one of the Canaries)
18 Nationality that seemingly boosts in population every March
19 Lots and lots
20 Bird of prey belonging to a peace goddess?
23 *Where Eagles Dare* novelist Alistair
25 Tomahawk look-alike
26 Cross-promotional ploys
27 Hawaiian goose that's a real drag?
32 Attendance check response
33 Subj. for green thumbs
35 One who flies solo, say
36 "Pay" ending that refers to bribery
37 Echoing birds
39 Flood-control org. established during the '30s
40 Deluxe pizza topping
42 Main squeeze, in Montreal
43 Hens and pens, e.g.
44 Those crazy for extinct birds?
46 Solid that has no sides
48 Some 45-Down ranks: Abbr.
49 Appeared first in the credits, say
50 President Clinton paired with a crazy bird?
55 Orchestra tuning instrument
56 Rock concert venue
57 Second word of *Chicken Little*
60 Collection of quails
61 They keep the blood flowing
62 Just-for-show model
63 Canonized women: Abbr.
64 Samuel Alito or Sonia Sotomayor, in college
65 Air Force NCO

DOWN

1 AP rival
2 Energy drink brand that sounds like denials
3 Speakeasy owner's worry
4 Jazz legend Parker, nicknamed "Bird"
5 Waters that surround Taiwan, China
6 Sophia who was the first Oscar winner whose performance was not English-speaking
7 Guitar legend Clapton
8 Looped handle (anagram of NASA)
9 1979 Revolution city
10 Drug that only works if you think it does
11 Pro ___ (proportionately)
12 Olfactory displeasure
13 Echoing bird
21 Day's end, to Donne
22 Ice dancing coups
23 Oregon's highest point, briefly
24 Danny of *Hudson Hawk*
27 Standards
28 Imaginary race for H. G. Wells
29 Close to defeat, like a boxer
30 Worship
31 Stricken from the record
34 Tag for Dixie- or techno-
37 Five: Prefix
38 It may set a legal precedent
41 Back-and-forth actions that may end in a smashing success?
43 Hides from view
45 Mil. branch whose seal features a bald eagle on an anchor
47 Golf great Se Ri ___
49 Muslim branch
50 Flappers' hairstyles
51 Skeptical remark
52 Turtledoves may represent it
53 De Matteo of *The Sopranos*
54 Cover overhead?
58 Twitter follower's surprised letters
59 The N of NIMBY

Answers on page 47

HAT CHECK
Presenting a stitched-together theme.

ACROSS

1 Door frame part
5 Worthless crud
10 Like pigeons
15 "That makes it clearer"
16 "Snowman," in poker lingo
17 Cheap white wine named for a German river
18 *Black-and-orange team named for a state bird
21 *Look Who's Talking ___* (1990 sequel)
22 It provides cover from the rain
23 Mattress support
24 *With 51-Across, lone Canadian MLB franchise
28 Vince's duet partner on the 1993 country hit "The Heart Won't Lie"
30 Fiscal periods: Abbr.
31 With strong resistance
33 Pulitzer-winner for Edna Ferber
35 Candy heart word of affection
36 Spot for flocks
38 Like Ford Thunderbirds, now
40 *Major leaguers depicted in *Major League*
46 Lose bit by bit
47 ___ Diego Chicken
48 Realm whose coat of arms depicted a Quaternion Eagle: Abbr.
49 Flashy jewelry, slangily
51 See 24-Across
55 Olympic gymnasts may fudge it
57 A gull's are webbed
59 Doesn't do any fact-checking
60 Falconry decoy
62 Takes after Jay-Z
64 Flight posting, for short
65 Good thing to have . . . and a uniform feature of the answers to the starred clues?
71 The Jetsons' pet
72 Make used to
73 "It can't be!"
74 Challenging for a rock climber
75 Red-ink ledger entry
76 Dark period, in ads

DOWN

1 Arm of a crane
2 Dumb ___ dodo
3 Voice of Daffy and Tweety
4 Player of the ponies
5 Knock down a rung on the corporate ladder
6 *Flying Down to ___*
7 Picture book baddie
8 Take off on the lamb?
9 Wood-burning heat sources
10 Temple Owls' conf. rival from Kingston
11 Greek P's
12 Graduate of the Florida Bible Institute in 1940
13 Lend ___ (listen)
14 Rookery residences
19 Particles with a charge
20 Like a phoenix from the ashes
24 Softest mineral
25 Very small egg
26 Bounce back, as sound
27 Casa crockpot
29 Tucked in, say
32 Deep desires
34 "Lord, is ___?" (question in Matthew)
37 Tiny bit of hair gel
39 How turkey is served for a Rachel sandwich
41 U. of Tennessee athlete
42 Fix some tpyos, say (speaking of which . . .)
43 "The Raven" heroine
44 *To Live and Die ___*
45 Legislative period: Abbr.
50 Made preparations, with "up"
52 Web discussion system first started in 1979
53 Right, on Canary Islands maps
54 Baptist college in Elgin, Illinois
55 Turin-manufactured cars, for short
56 One sleeping over for the night
58 A chicken lacks one
61 French 101 verb
63 Dis by not mentioning
66 Quick flight
67 "Either I get a raise, ___ quit!"
68 Blackhawks, on scoreboards
69 Insect eaten by hummingbirds
70 "The Raven" writer

Answers on page 47

SOFT SPOT
Get a warm and fuzzy feeling from this one.

ACROSS

1 ["Your fly is open"]
5 Receptacle for grounds
8 Builds a wing, perhaps
14 Become morose
16 Scissor-___ flycatcher (bird also known as a Texas bird-of-paradise)
17 Honey pie, turtledove, etc.
18 Have in mind
19 1936 also-ran Landon
20 Post-bathing powder
22 Linguist's suffix
23 "That's a major buzzkill, bro"
27 Not as cheap
29 Need an ice pack, maybe
30 Win in a walk
32 ___ Lanka
33 Org. for patriotic ladies
34 Fit to ___
35 It may tell you that the bird cage needs to be cleaned
38 "Telephone Line" gp.
39 Mid-'80s marketing disaster
41 Slimy stuff
42 Buffet-style seafood joint
44 Make flight difficult, as with a bird's wings
45 Shell out for
46 One shaking hands and kissing babies, for short
47 Journey to 31-Down
48 It's between Oscar and Quebec in the NATO alphabet
49 Kenya's largest city
52 "Brutish" Oliver Stone film of 2012
54 Right-angled joint
55 Slimy stuff
57 Daffy Duck collectible
58 Enter a car en masse
60 High-pH battery type
65 Made up for past transgressions
66 Compact item applied on a lid
67 Like the nethermost regions
68 Result of a serve that hits the net, maybe
69 Duck's material that the answers to the starred clues can be made of . . . or the orientation of those answers in the grid

DOWN

1 The Eiger in Switzerland, for one
2 Green thumb's implement
3 Clock setting for Penguins games, for short
4 Osprey, to fish
5 *Bed spread
6 Talk like a cockatiel
7 A pheasant's is called a nide
8 On a slant
9 Salsa component?
10 Morse code click
11 *Accommodation in a tent
12 With one's blood up
13 Less conventional
15 Wings' go-with for an angelic costume
21 Symbol for a pharaoh
23 Seat belt advocate Ralph
24 Central city in the Sunshine State
25 *You can put your head on one
26 MGM co-founder Marcus
28 Prior to, in poems
31 Holy city in Islam
34 SAT section
35 *Wear for one doing a spread eagle
36 Two-door hatchback, e.g.
37 Golden Eagles' Big East rival from Georgetown
40 Starfire maker
43 One of five in N.Y.C.
47 Strawberry Kiwi Kraze brand
48 Sickly looking
49 Its national bird is the Himalayan monal
50 Samuel who started a job for life in 2005
51 ___ cake (ring-shaped goodie)
53 Osso buco meat
56 Pauline who panned *The Birds*
59 San Diego-to-Phoenix dir.
61 Cleaning agent in soap
62 Cadmus' daughter (found in BINOCULARS)
63 Unlike a rerun
64 Marine eagle: Var.

Answers on page 48

AERIAL ATTACK
Have pun, will travel.

ACROSS

1 Bogart's one-time squeeze
7 Narrow naval passage
10 Chicken nuggets go-with, briefly
14 Result in
15 Hawkeyes' conf. rival
16 Ample, old-style
17 High-pitched shorebird gone mad?
19 Showroom Firebird, perhaps
20 Eagle-like Garuda of Hindu mythology, for one
21 Opera refashioned by Tim Rice and Elton John
22 Old Houston athlete
23 Orange-red Australian passerine gone mad?
27 Some chicken wing bones
29 California beachside community
30 With 47-Across, long-legged wader gone mad?
32 63-Across target
33 Far from fat
37 Bring-along to a yoga class
38 Jayhawk's term, for short
40 Wrap alternative
42 It feminizes "señor"
43 Cochran's appeal
45 Highlander's turndown
47 See 30-Across
49 Throwing a party in honor of
52 Ernie the Giant Chicken, to Peter Griffin
53 Pennsylvania state bird gone mad?
57 Parroting types
58 Merit, or a homophone of a seabird
59 Some 12-Steppers, briefly
62 Mallet sport
63 Popular iPhone game . . . and an alternate title for this puzzle
66 Aware of
67 World Cup cry
68 Dethroning event
69 Imperfection on an AMC Eagle
70 Thomas who some say Shakespeare stole from
71 Orrin Hatch et al.

DOWN

1 *The Perch* on the Audubon Society's website, for one
2 Flying start?
3 One running for office
4 Larkspur offering, once
5 PO box item
6 Like an Eagle Scout
7 Glove box reference
8 Tel Aviv natives
9 Penguin's relative that can fly
10 Like assembly-line work, to some
11 Suet package weight, maybe
12 Marisa of *Cyrus*
13 Like a stool pigeon's in-court testimony
18 He played Oskar in *Schindler's List*
22 Globe, e.g.
24 Beak of a bird
25 Small cock-and-bull stories
26 Excavate by shovel
27 Cops in Alberta, for short
28 Contracting Asian sea
31 Matchmaker of Broadway fame
34 2007 concert event founded by Al Gore
35 Bullet point
36 Actress Ure of *Where Eagles Dare*
39 Befitting of a young girl
41 Chicken wing cheese
44 Shot to one's ego
46 Like some lovebirds
48 Carry-___ (some flight baggage)
50 2012 British Open champ Ernie
51 Guard dog's warning
53 Like a hummingbird
54 Leading 5–4, say
55 The Birdman from Alcatraz, for one
56 "The joke's ___!"
60 Yemeni port
61 Former protectorates: Abbr.
63 Pilot's "jake"
64 On the other hand
65 Tom Cochrane's "Life ___ Highway"

Answers on page 46

FROM SIDE TO SIDE
A new take on a classic set-up.

ACROSS

1 "Mockingbird" and "Blackbird," for two
6 Pump name in Winnipeg
10 Sushi seed
16 Ahead by a point, say
17 ___ helmet (jungle headwear)
18 Latin for "and others"
19 "The Raven" writer, for short
20 Break room notice heading
21 Start of a classic riddle involving the circled squares
22 Part 2 of the riddle
24 *Little Birds* writer Nin
25 Trig function
26 Spicy green chili pepper
29 [See riddle]
33 Mast ropes
34 "I'm Yours" hitmaker Jason, 2008
38 "___ saw Elba"
39 DDE's two-time opponent
41 Donald Duck's "miserly" uncle
43 The N of NCO
44 End of the riddle
47 After nightfall, in Nantes
50 Once around the track
51 Pigeonhole's place
52 Start of the riddle's answer
57 Turkey Day, e.g.: Abbr.
59 Free jazz pioneer Coleman
60 Not optional: Abbr.
61 Woodpecker's "money maker"
62 Rick with the 1976 hit "Disco Duck"
63 Coup d'___
66 Swiss canton or its capital
68 Falcon noted for swooping down on its prey
71 Charged particle
72 "Are you calling me ___?"
75 End of the riddle's answer
80 Coop youngster
82 Eastern tongue that gave us "typhoon"
83 Do a doorman's job, maybe
84 Swallow
85 Flip a lid
86 Bird guide preface
87 Gives one a hard time
88 Canadian coins with loons on them
89 Approaches, as time

DOWN

1 Cake for a bird
2 Flashy aquarium swimmer
3 "'Fraid not"
4 Italian counterpart to Polish *kopytka* dumplings
5 Comprehend
6 Light reading it's not
7 Washroom array
8 [See riddle]
9 Writer with a short story prize named for him
10 Be a pedal pusher, perhaps
11 Hawke of *A Midnight Clear*
12 "Consider it done"
13 He succeeded Sutherland playing Hawkeye Pierce
14 1003, in old Rome
15 Bridge architect of St. Louis fame
23 Hayes in *Robin Hood: Men in Tights*
27 Take a break from migrating, say
28 *The Nazarene* author Sholem
29 Mother clucker
30 Resource heavily mined in northern Minnesota
31 Not a fake
32 "___ Blues" (Beatles tune)
35 Cock-y fella?
36 Islamic pooh-bah
37 One of two in a British buzzard?
40 *Storage Wars* word
42 Like the northern cardinal
45 Eagle of the Muppets
46 Practice some hooks and jabs
48 Footwear for Penguins
49 Big Bird fan, often
52 Grass that's rolled up
53 Beehive State athletes
54 Native Latvian
55 *Kenan & ___* ('90s comedy show)
56 Get ready for camping
58 Beach party strings, perhaps
61 Compound found in crude oil
64 ___ Fuente (White Owl cigars competitor)
65 Capital city for Ahmadinejad
67 Fethry Duck, to Donald Duck
69 Use a butt end of a pencil
70 Former Phillies All-Star closer Brad
72 One iota
73 [See riddle]
74 Swenson of *The Miracle Worker*
76 Slaps a suit on, say
77 Z on sororities
78 Train that runs to Jamaica (N.Y., that is)
79 Cardinals Hall-of-Famer Slaughter
81 Chain of peaks, for short

Answers on page 47

COLORFUL OPENING
Make a flashy entrance with this one.

ACROSS

1 Like an occasion to wear a penguin suit
7 Vowel salesman Sajak
10 Certain spa pampering, for short
14 Blob under a microscope
15 Long-necked bird Down Under
16 Model that features Safari
17 Remove by a spade, perhaps
18 *2009 animated film based on a Neil Gaiman novel
20 *Egyptian site of a noted 1799 discovery
22 Pan for a fry cook
23 With 65-Across, Italian operatic standard
25 Ranch addition?
26 Quite a ways away
29 *Grade-school promise
34 Fatty acids, e.g.
36 Chicken pox symptom
37 Health woe sometimes transmitted by birds
38 Physical strength
39 Happy-as-a-lark feeling
40 Awards for plays not on the "Great White Way"
42 Groove-billed cuckoo
43 Game with a straight-rail variant
45 Quantity in many an egg carton
46 *Bacteria from chickens
49 Goes out with socially
50 Take advantage of
51 Bird's instruments
53 Pursuing a wild goose?
57 *Crisp apple variety
61 Colorful songbird . . . and a description of the answers to the starred clues?
63 Young players that show promise
64 Jay Gould's railroad, named for a Great Lake
65 See 23-Across
66 Says "Duck!," perhaps
67 Begin a game of Rook
68 Pro who may legally drive through stop signs: Abbr.
69 Smaller cousin to a toucan

DOWN

1 Jamie who played The Sheik in *Cannonball Run*
2 Melville novel featuring a mutiny
3 Pocketed hoppers, for short
4 Swift, like one's rise to fame
5 Leans up against
6 Notebooks that contain no paper?
7 Gym rat's pride
8 Minor prophet after Joel
9 They're often stuffed with aromatics
10 It's often stuffed with eider down
11 Donald Duck foe ___ Eagle
12 Queen Margrethe II, for one
13 Rapper who sounds like an Arnold Palmer ingredient
19 Impressive flight display
21 MacGraw once married to McQueen
24 Registers for a course
26 Some sporty imports, for short
27 Singer Apple who once advocated for PETA
28 One of Daisy Duck's nieces
30 "Every kiss begins with ___" (jewelry jingle)
31 Save a stamp during tax time, say
32 Headache-easing brand
33 Sneaky maneuvers
35 It's a plus on the balance sheet
39 Torre who won the 1971 NL MVP for the Cardinals
41 Eponymous steel magnate Henry
44 What Drake and Falco use
45 One that frequently leaves LAX
47 Cioppino ingredient
48 Legal eagle's expertise
52 ___ Gay
53 Rep on the street
54 Not over there
55 Hit McLachlan ballad
56 Not looking good for the future
58 Balkan Wars fighter
59 *Laugh-In* comedian Johnson
60 [Hey you, over there]
62 Carpet crawler

Answers on page 46

BONUS ROUND
Oh I almost forgot . . .

ACROSS

1 Groundhogs and such
8 Bill holder, for short
11 It's precious for a Mexican miner
14 Parent's stern warning
15 Caught some z's, say
17 *Soft drink for an *Arabian Nights* bird?
18 Take off the table, as an offer
19 ___ *Grit* (western featuring Rooster Cogburn)
20 *With 43-Across, jailbird's provisions include some owlish sounds plus one black water bird?
22 Pronoun for Polly
23 Chicken salad seller
24 Not too many
25 Word repeated before "robin" in a Jolson standard
26 Newborn not yet at home
31 Fred's wife on *I Love Lucy*
34 *The Cardinal* director Preminger
35 ___ tai
36 *Alt rockers feature a pink bird's kissers?
40 Goose egg
41 Cornmeal cake
42 Charge towards
43 *See 20-Across
46 Frat party centerpiece
47 Bird feeder morsel
48 Agenda point
50 It sticks to feathers
53 *Silent horror star gone mad?
57 "___ Blue Eyes" (Velvet Underground hit)
58 Certain engine air lines
59 Small passerine . . . and a homophone that explains the feature added to the answers to the starred clues
61 Nature-lover's college major
62 Inside track position
63 "You dig?"
64 Cockney's residence
65 Brought home a pet parrot, say

DOWN

1 High spirits
2 Italian word in the title of a Dean Martin hit
3 Rear its ugly head, again
4 Mist you don't want in your eyes
5 Musician with the 1972 Lennon-produced album *Fly*
6 Like a table with a short leg
7 *60 Minutes* correspondent Leslie
8 Sanctuary unit
9 Amphibian who may build a nest
10 Prepares potatoes, in a way
11 Where to find a college town called Oxford
12 Collegian's expense
13 An underdog has long ones
16 Disgusted look
21 Movie star "discovered" on a World War I battlefield
23 "The Farmer in the ___"
25 Zebra that may penalize a Seahawk
27 Alt-weekly founder Eric
28 "You've sold me"
29 Valley that served as the setting for *Falcon Crest*
30 Basic premise
31 Active Italian volcano
32 Crispy pizza crust choice
33 Kept a grip on
34 Melville classic
37 Well-worn phrase
38 Provo neighbor
39 Clumsy dodo
44 Yearly recap
45 Bird that announces the time, in kitschy clocks
46 Touchtone phone component
49 Electricity scientist Nikola
50 Occultist's deck
51 By itself
52 Said "'til death do us part" to a second person, say
53 Isn't straight with
54 2012 Tony-winning musical
55 Chief Whitehorse was one
56 ". . . so long ___ shall live?"
57 Do KP work, briefly
60 Enero starts it

Answers on page 46

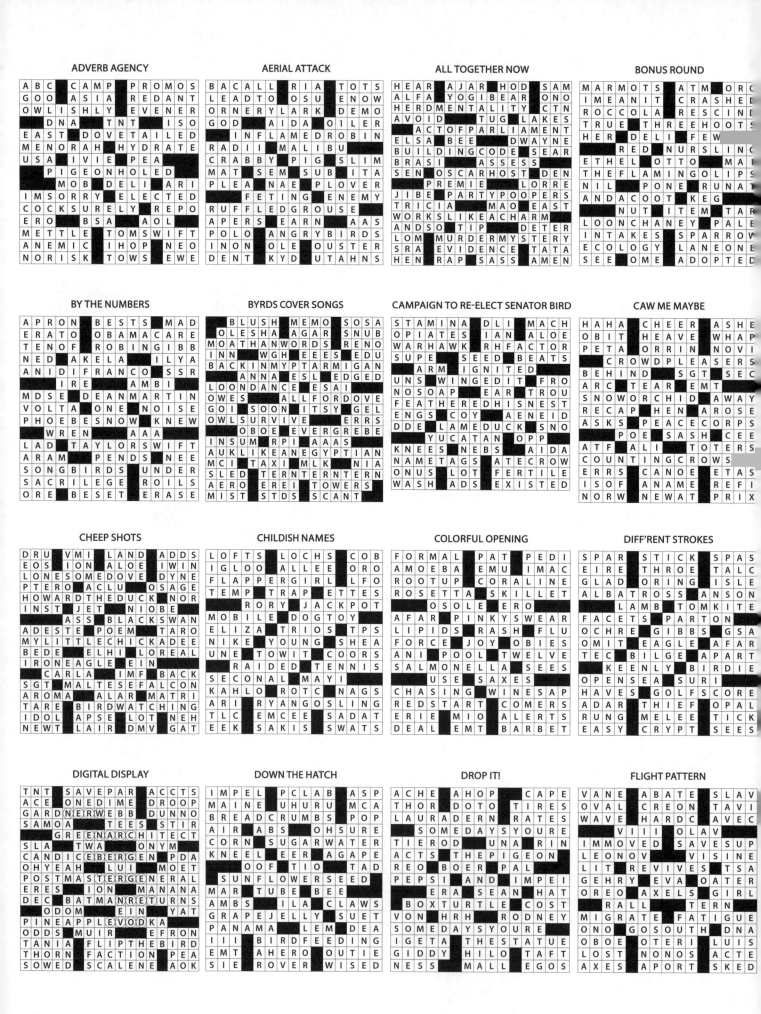

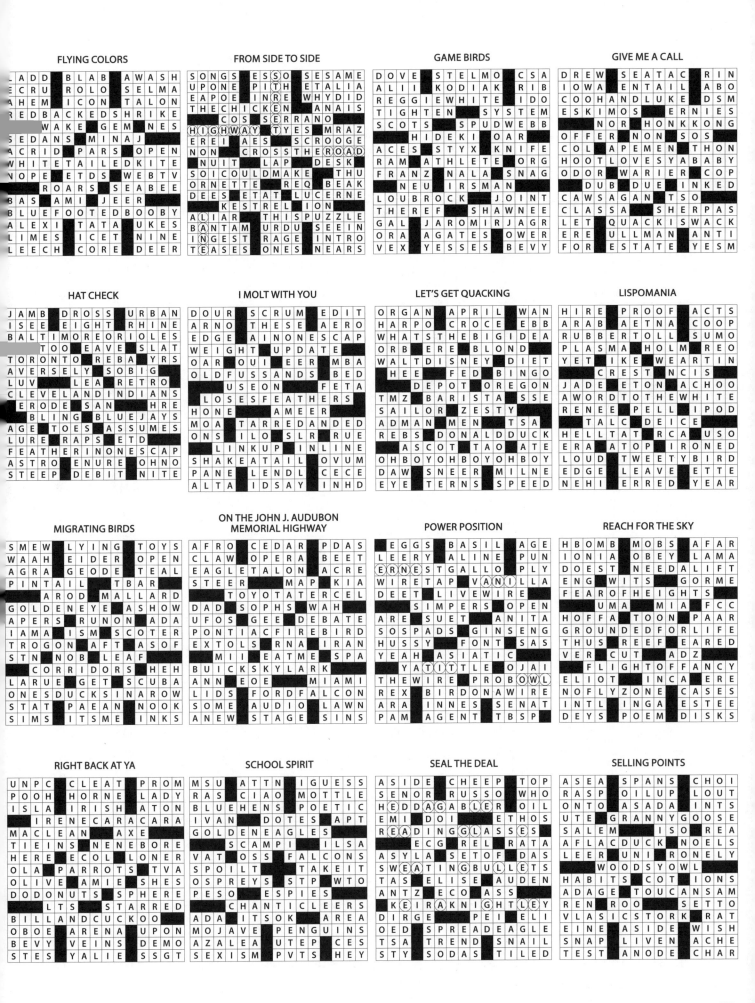

FLYING COLORS

FROM SIDE TO SIDE

GAME BIRDS

GIVE ME A CALL

HAT CHECK

I MOLT WITH YOU

LET'S GET QUACKING

LISPOMANIA

MIGRATING BIRDS

ON THE JOHN J. AUDUBON MEMORIAL HIGHWAY

POWER POSITION

REACH FOR THE SKY

RIGHT BACK AT YA

SCHOOL SPIRIT

SEAL THE DEAL

SELLING POINTS

SERVICE WITH A SIMILE

SOFT SPOT

STUCK IN THE MIDDLE

SYMBOLIC FLIERS

THE BIRDS AND THE B'S

THIS BIRD'S FOR HUE

TOMFOOLERY

TWEET-Y BIRDS

ABOUT THE AUTHOR

Andrew J. Ries is a lifelong resident of Minnesota. He was raised in Hastings, a quiet Twin Cities suburb on the Mississippi River and moved to St. Cloud in order to attend college at St. Cloud State University. After graduating with a bachelor's degree in history and film studies, Ries decided to stay in St. Cloud, and it was in 2009 that he published his first crossword book, *Minnesota Crosswords*. His second book, *Michigan Crosswords*, was released in 2011.

Crossword puzzles have long been a passion for Ries. He remembers first working puzzles with his grandmother when he was five years old. By the time high school came, Ries began to solve the *New York Times* crossword puzzle seriously, and by the time he graduated from high school, he was an able and proficient solver. These skills were honed by doing more and more puzzles (and gaining much more useless knowledge along the way), and starting in 2009, he took those skills to New York City to compete in the American Crossword Puzzle Tournament. His best finish at the tournament was 41st in 2011.

Ries began constructing puzzles in 2006 and had his first published puzzle run in *The New York Times* on August 13, 2007. His puzzles have also run in various newspapers, magazines and books across the country. In 2010, he launched his own website and he offers free crosswords and variety puzzles on a weekly basis there. Visit his site at www.ariespuzzles.com.

Aside from crosswords, Ries is an avid sports fan, loves going to the movies, and enjoys listening to a wide variety of music. He holds season tickets to the St. Cloud State University Husky hockey team and doesn't miss a game. He also competes in a local cribbage league and plays the piano.